CRUX

CRUX

A Quarterly Journal of Christian Thought and Opinion published by Regent College

CRUX, a journal of Christian thought and opinion, seeks to expound the basic tenets of the Christian faith and to demonstrate that Christian truth is relevant to the whole of life. Its particular concern is to relate the teachings of Scripture to a broad spectrum of academic, social, and professional areas of interest, to integrate them, and to apply the insights gained to corporate and personal Christian life and witness.

Founded in 1962 by the Toronto Graduate Christian Fellowship and subsequently published by a group of Christian faculty members associated with Scarborough College in the University of Toronto, **CRUX** has been published since 1979 by Faculty and Alumni of Regent College, Vancouver, BC, Canada.

Views expressed in **CRUX** should be regarded as the personal opinions of the individual authors rather than as reflecting the official opinions or policies of Regent College.

Articles appearing in this journal are abstracted and indexed in *Religious and Theological Abstracts, Old Testament Abstracts, New Testament Abstracts,* and *Religion Index One.*

This periodical is indexed in the *ATLA Religion Database,* published by the American Theological Library Association, 250 S. Wacker Drive, 16th Floor, Chicago, IL 60606. Email: atla@atla.com, website: www.atla.com.

Subscriptions: CAD/USD$26 for one year, CAD/USD$49 for two years, and CAD/USD$72 for three years. CAD/USD$7 for single copies. (For Canadian subscribers, please add the applicable HST/GST to the total amount.)

Payments by credit cards or cheques are accepted. Cheques should be made out to Regent College.

All editorial correspondence, notices of change of subscription address, and financial contributions to help defray the cost of publication should be sent to:

CRUX **Circulation Department**
Regent College
5800 University Boulevard
Vancouver, BC, Canada V6T 2E4

Books for review should be sent to:

CRUX **Book Review Editor**
Regent College
5800 University Boulevard
Vancouver, BC Canada V6T 2E4

ISSN 0011-2186
ISBN 978-1-57383-458-2

Contents

CRUX: Fall 2012/Vol. 48, No. 3

A Quarterly Journal of Christian Thought and Opinion published by Regent College

ARTICLES

Front Cover: James M. Houston, founding principal of Regent College, is pictured here giving a convocation address around the year 1980.

Back Cover: Diane Stinton's article explores the theme of reconciliation through a case study of one particular community of refugee women in Nairobi: Amani ya Juu. Their "Unity Quilt" celebrates traditional reconciliation rituals from their various people groups, but also looks toward a more lasting solution, the hope and peace only possible through Christ's work on the cross. Photo by Diane Stinton, used with permission from Amani ya Juu.

Introduction:
A Festschrift for James M. Houston

It is with a great deal of pleasure that we introduce you to a departure from the usual format of *Crux*. The present issue has been created entirely in honour of Dr. James M. Houston. As Regent's founding principal, Dr. Houston has had an unprecedented influence on countless Regent students over the last fifty years. This issue is what academics warmly call a Festschrift—translated as "celebration writing"—and here we celebrate Jim Houston's upcoming ninetieth birthday on November 21, 2012. For this unique issue, Regent faculty members Hans Boersma, Craig Gay, and Bruce Hindmarsh have acted as guest editors for *Crux*, and we thank them for their varied, constant, and scholarly efforts.

—Julie Lane Gay

About James M. Houston

Jim Houston has had an outstanding career as a Christian educator, a public intellectual, a Christian statesman, and a spiritual director. Born in Scotland to Brethren missionary parents, Houston was educated at Edinburgh and Oxford. Before he came to Canada, he had a distinguished career as a geographer and historian of ideas (1947–1971) and wrote several highly respected books that were standard reading in his field. He was a senior fellow and bursar of Hertford College. A wide circle of Christian intellectuals met regularly in his home for discussion of religious topics, and his circle of friends included the Russian intellectual Nicholas Zernov, Malcolm Muggeridge, and C. S. Lewis.

Jim gave up the security of his academic career in Oxford in 1970 to become the founding principal of Regent College, and his vision shaped Regent as an international graduate school with a unique focus on lay theological education. In 1976 he also co-founded the C. S. Lewis Institute in Washington, DC, to bring Christian reflection to the domains of personal and public life in America's capital. His heart for the Christian laity is also reflected in the men's breakfast he has led in downtown Vancouver for over thirty years.

In addition to his work as an institutional founder and educational leader, Jim Houston has shown remarkable prescience in his intellectual career, alert to widespread changes in the culture and the need to be ahead of these trends as a Christian thinker. Early in his career at Regent, he focused on Christian epistemology and the Christian mind at a time when this emphasis was sorely needed among evangelicals. He also worked widely in environmental ethics and a theology of creation, long before this became fashionable. At the University of British Columbia, his students included some of the young activists who went on to found the first serious environmental advocacy organizations. In 1978, he moved into teaching and writing about spiritual theology—again, long before this was fashionable. He established the first program in spiritual theology in the evangelical world at Regent College, which very much addressed the needs of the hour for students.

Before anyone was using the word "postmodernism," Jim Houston was aware

CRUX: Fall 2012/Vol. 48, No. 3

that the rising generation needed to see the Christian mind as part of the response of the whole Christian person to God and his grace. His whole career was founded on this Christian personalism. This focus on persons stimulated not only a basic Christian humanism concerned with all of life under God, but also a personal approach to students and to everyone he meets. He has a generosity of spirit matched with a prophetic boldness to always speak honestly to the truth as he sees it. There are countless Christian men and women today whose lives have been changed by a single, never-to-be-forgotten conversation with Jim. Informally and formally, he became a spiritual director and mentor to a whole generation of students, and to hundreds of men and women around the world, through conversation and letter writing. His mentoring has included working personally with key educational and political leaders across North America and the Pacific Rim. Again, his focus on spiritual direction emerged at a time when this was a growing concern among many Jesuits, but long before evangelicals became interested.

Jim Houston's fluency in French meant that he was reading the *nouvelle* theologians about a generation before other evangelicals were, and he was therefore alert to the need to put students in touch with the early church fathers as a living tradition and source of renewal, long before the patristic revival became popular among evangelical theologians and publishers. His close relationship with the Torrance family in Scotland helped him be alert to the importance of trinitarian theology for Christian life and witness before the wider revival of trinitarian theology broke like a wave on these shores. Even now he continues as a pioneer, thinking and writing about aging, and the implications for the church of the demographic changes that are coming and about the imperative of a new Christian culture of care.

As a Christian intellectual and educator, Jim has meaningfully integrated an unusual breadth of interdisciplinary reading and insight; he has spoken prophetically to the secularization and depersonalization of human life in Western culture and the church; and he has awakened a whole generation of evangelicals to the much neglected, larger heritage of Christian spirituality. And he is still going strong. In May of this year he was presented with a lifetime achievement award from Christian Higher Education Canada in recognition of his outstanding contribution to Christian education in Canada and around the world.

On the occasion of his ninetieth birthday, we thought it appropriate to draw attention to Jim Houston's legacy by inviting a few scholars of the next generation to write essays in his honour. His peers have written on his behalf in previous Festschriften, but now it is the turn of his younger colleagues and friends. Jim has been concerned throughout his career with paradosis, the handing on of a living faith to the next generation. All those of us who have written here bear witness to the fruitfulness of his life and of his commitment to the personal in all dimensions of faith and life. We present these essays in gratitude for Jim's influence in each of our lives and with our love and best wishes on his ninetieth birthday.

Hans Boersma
Craig Gay
Bruce Hindmarsh

"The God of Nature and of Grace": Early Evangelical Spirituality and Reflection on Nature

Bruce Hindmarsh

Bruce Hindmarsh is the James M. Houston Professor of Spiritual Theology at Regent College.

Although known for his pioneering contribution to spiritual theology among evangelicals for over three decades, Jim Houston was never one to conceive of spirituality as something private that could be somehow independent of how one thinks about everything else. One of the first books by Jim that I read was his *I Believe in the Creator* (1979), which outlined a thoughtful theology of creation long before environmental concerns became popular. For years he also taught a course at Regent on "The Christian Mind" that helped students develop a Christian worldview and epistemology. Even his courses on spiritual theology, such as "The Christian Spirit," which were some of the first courses of this kind in any evangelical college or seminary in North America, were originally offered as part of the wider curriculum of interdisciplinary studies at Regent, where connections were made across disciplines in the effort to think Christianly about all of life.

I present the following essay to Jim as one more exploration of the relationship between spirituality and the rest of life. Much of my research has focused on the rise of evangelicalism in the eighteenth century, and so I would like to ask how the early evangelical leaders such as John and Charles Wesley or Jonathan Edwards located their evangelical piety within a wider picture of the world. To make a beginning on this question, my essay will focus chiefly on one little-known poem by Charles Wesley, which begins addressing God as the "Author of every work divine, / Who dost through both creations shine, / The God of nature and of grace."

In 1745 and 1746, Charles Wesley published a number of hymnbooks related to liturgical themes and the liturgical calendar. The full title of his *Whitsundtide* or *Pentecost* hymnbook was *Hymns of Petition and Thanksgiving for the Promise of the Father* (1746)—hymns, that is, to the promised Holy Spirit. Most of the hymns invoke the Spirit to make personal the work of Christ for the believer, but Hymn 28 takes a wider view of the work of the Spirit in creation and re-creation. Stanza 1 describes the Spirit as the author of every work divine, who shines with a transfiguring light through both the original creation and the redeemed creation.

> Author of every work Divine,
> Who dost through both creations
>   shine,
> The God of nature and of grace,
> Thy glorious steps in all we see,
> And wisdom attribute to Thee,
> And power, and majesty, and praise.[1]

The Holy Spirit is the same God of nature and of grace without division for Wesley. Not only does the Spirit irradiate or transfigure the old and new creation, as the disciples witnessed on Mount Tabor, but the Spirit also leaves traces of his work—"glorious steps"—that we may see in all his works, and so the one who discerns the Spirit in the history of the universe as in the history of redemption attributes to the Spirit the fourfold characteristics of wisdom, power, majesty, and praise. Wesley is nothing if not biblical, saturated as he was in the Scriptures, and these attributes were by no means random. *Sophia, dunamis, doxa*—these are throughout the New Testament the words most associated with the Spirit. Gordon Fee has taught us that *dunamis*, or power, is often used synecdochely for the Spirit in the letters of St. Paul. When St. Paul writes of power, he means, most often, the Holy Spirit. Wesley seemed to understand this instinctively, and he hymns the Spirit accordingly.

In a dense second stanza, Wesley compresses his account of the original creation in Genesis, as the Spirit broods over the chaos and creates ex nihilo.

> Thou didst Thy mighty wings
> outspread,
> And brooding o'er the chaos, shed
> Thy life into the impregn'd abyss,
> The vital principle infuse,
> And out of nothing's womb produce
> The earth and heaven, and all that is.

The language of pregnancy and womb here are combined with the traditional ex nihilo doctrine in a daring way. This is no fertility myth or doctrine of emanation, and Charles Wesley distinguishes clearly between the created and the uncreated, but nonetheless he communicates the intimate bond of love between the Creator and the creation. That the hovering Spirit "shed" his life into the impregn'd abyss suggests already a kind of suffering maternal love. And the language of "vital principle" recalls a Paracelsian sense of the immanence of the divine life as the animating centre of the material world. The word "vital" does not, of course, as in our own everyday usage, simply mean important, but is the adjective for the Latin *vita,* or life. The Holy Spirit thus animates the world as an infused, principial life force.

Reg Ward argues that in the German evangelical tradition this appreciation of the universe as animated by divine life was all but universal. When Pietists sought to renew religious vitality in their churches, they understood this as in direct continuity with the cosmic principle of life that they saw in the Paracelsian, alchemical outlook that they inherited from the Renaissance in which medicine, astrology, botany, and chemistry were all bound together in a hermetical belief in the spiritual character of the universe. The life within and the life without were the same; this was simply another aspect of the human as a microcosm of the universe. The same Spirit was at work in the microcosm as in the macrocosm, as in Wesley's hymn. Indeed, Ward makes "vitalism" one of the hallmarks of the whole German evangelical tradition as it emerges in the late seventeenth and early eighteenth century. "The vitalism that characterized the whole alchemical tradition," he writes, "was a clear attraction to men like Arndt and the Pietists of a later generation who were seeking to recover religious vitality."[2] In this hymn by Charles Wesley it is clear, however, that this cosmological vital principle was equated not with some cabbalistic, hermetic Neoplatonism, as it could be in some esoteric religious traditions, but with the biblical Holy Spirit.

The following stanza extends this sense of the Holy Spirit of God as the life of the world under the image of inspiration:

> That all-informing breath Thou art
> Who dost continued life impart,
> And bidd'st the world persist to be.

The Spirit is thus critical not just to the original creation at the beginning but also to the sustaining of the world. The continuing action of the Holy Spirit to will the persistence of the world echoes the occasionalism and doctrine of continuous creation in Jonathan Edwards: every moment of the universe depends wholly on the bidding of the Spirit. In Wesley's hymn, the image of the Spirit as the interior life of the world is balanced in the last half of this stanza by the picture of the transcendent Spirit holding the stars and planets, suspending them by golden filaments.

> Garnish'd by Thee yon azure sky,
> And all those beauteous orbs on high
> Depend in golden chains from Thee.

The "golden chains" that hold the universe in suspension, like the divine breath that gives life to the world, describe a reality that is not in any way autonomous, reduced to the operation of abstract law or to material properties and mechanical operations as was becoming much more common in the Enlightenment. Wesley's use of the verb "depend" expresses not only contingency in the abstract but also the notion of hanging, like one might hang a picture. The "beauteous orbs on high" thus depend utterly and entirely upon the Spirit for their moment-by-moment existence. The universe is suspended from an Archimedean point in God himself; the universe is not an independent sphere. Yet, although the Spirit is the immanent life of the world, he also transcends it.

The theme of continuous creation is sustained in the fourth stanza, where nature is described not as blind and mute but as responsive to the Spirit of God, perceiving the Spirit's motions and acknowledging the Spirit's governance:

> Thou dost create the earth anew,
> (Its Maker and Preserver too,)
> By Thine almighty arm sustain:
> Nature perceives Thy secret force,
> And still holds on her even course,
> And owns Thy providential reign.

The conceit, if it is a conceit, that nature perceives the Spirit's motions and responds consciously to obey and acknowledge his lordship suggests a dynamic view of nature as capable of answering in some way to God, just as the psalmist describes the heavens "declaring" the glory of God.

Boldly, Charles Wesley draws on the language of Plotinus and Neoplatonism—but without a hint of a demiurgic doctrine of emanation—when he continues, addressing the Spirit in the next stanza:

> Thou art the Universal Soul,
> The plastic power that fills the whole,
> And governs earth, air, sea, and sky.

What Wesley writes here echoes Alexander Pope, who said similarly, "All are but parts of one stupendous Whole, / Whose body Nature is, and God the soul."3 Charles Wesley returns to the central image of divine breath:

> The creatures all Thy breath
>   receive,
> And who by Thy inspiring live,
> Without Thy inspiration die.

Far from reflecting an uncritical Platonism in his reference to the "Universal Soul," Wesley echoes the Psalter's language about creaturely dependence upon the breath of God. The whole poem could be seen as a commentary on Psalm 104, and here especially the verses "When thou takest away their breath they die, and are turned again to their dust. When thou lettest thy breath go forth they shall be made: and thou shalt renew the face of the earth" (Ps. 104:29–30, *Book of Common Prayer* [1662]).

Clearly, Charles Wesley believed that the being of the natural world was contingent at every moment and in every place upon the divine life. The world is distinct from God, but its being derives wholly from God, who remains as closely knit to the creation as soul to body. The Spirit is the "vital principle" of all created being, without whom it ceases to be. The creation thus participates in God while remaining distinct from God.

Finally, in the last stanza, Wesley returns to his more usual theme of the work of the Spirit of God in the redemption of humankind. It is this same immense God, this eternal nous, who works to save the lost and redeem the world.

> Spirit immense, eternal Mind,
> Thou on the souls of lost mankind
> Dost with benignest influence move,
> Pleased to restore the ruin'd race,
> And new-create a world of grace
> In all the image of Thy love.

The conclusion of this poem could not be more clear in describing the work of salvation in terms that go back to Irenaeus as a work to "restore" or recapitulate the original creation. The restoration of the human race involves a new creation of a world of grace, or, as it is put in Romans 8, a sharing of the creation in the liberty and glory of the children of God. To be thus remade in the image of God is to be remade also in the image of the Spirit of God as the eternal and incessant love that binds the Father and the Son. It is, as this hymn concludes, to be created anew in all the image of divine love.

One might worry that the emphasis of this poem could blur the distinction between God and the world, but it is clear from other poems that Wesley affirmed just as robustly the infinite dissimilarity between the creation and the Creator. The being of the world was neither equivocal nor univocal when compared to God's own being; it was analogical. Although human persons were made for a divine end, and the new-created world with them, this divine end surpassed all human comprehension. And so, in another hymn to the Spirit, Wesley invokes the Spirit to come and dwell within his own soul, to prepare and consecrate his soul as a temple, as the apostle Paul described it.

> Come, Holy Ghost, all-quick'ning
>   fire,
> Come, and in me delight to rest!
> Drawn by the lure of strong desire,
> O come, and consecrate my breast:
> The temple of my soul prepare,
> And fix thy sacred presence there![4]

The Universal Soul that in the first poem fills the whole of earth, air, sea, and sky is invoked here to fill the human heart. The "vital principle" that in the first poem was cosmological is here the "principle divine" that properly animates the Christian soul and excites its desire to be united with the Godhead in love. And so Wesley continues:

> Eager for thee I ask and pant,
> So strong the principle divine
> Carries me out with sweet constraint,
> Till all my hallowed soul be thine:
> Plunged in the Godhead's deepest sea,
> And lost in thy immensity.

There is often in Charles Wesley this recognition of God's immensity and our corresponding experience of vertigo, which he typically signals, as he does here, with the word "lost." The believer recognizes her own finitude and the infinitude of God for which she is made. It is the very deepest of seas, and even as one enters in, one is lost. As he says elsewhere, "lost in wonder, love and praise," disoriented by the vastness of the divine life and the greatness of divine love.

The metaphysic that goes along with modernity typically treated the natural world as autonomous, and while lip service may have been paid for a time to its divine origin, natural philosophy even during Charles Wesley's lifetime increasingly explained the world without invoking supernatural agency. For all that John Wesley may have celebrated the findings of early modern science or natural philosophy, and commended these to others in writings such as his *Survey of the Wisdom of God in Creation* (1763), the language of his science as of his hymnody and worship was, like that of his brother Charles, not of a univocity of being. He distinguished carefully between the description of appearances and the accounting for things themselves. This latter knowledge was too profound for human ingenuity: "In many cases we cannot know; and the more we enquire, the more we are perplext and intangled. *God hath so done his Works,* that we may admire and adore."[5] It was the wisdom of God that he saw in his survey of natural philosophy. The visible creation had an entelechy and ought to be seen, said Wesley, "directed to its right End." Science ought "not barely to entertain an idle, barren Curiosity, but to display *the invisible things of God,* his Power, Wisdom and Goodness."[6] Indeed, Wesley closed his preface to this compendium

For all that John Wesley may have celebrated the findings of early modern science … his hymnody and worship was, like that of his brother Charles, not of a univocity of being.

of natural philosophy by invoking the same phrase that forms the climax of the hymn, "Love Divine, All Loves Excelling," writing that such science, by displaying the attributes of God, warms the heart and fills one with "Wonder, Love and Praise." The devotion apparent in Wesleyan hymnody easily passed over into an attitude of wonder in contemplation of the visible world revealed through natural philosophy and experimental science as it opened up and pointed toward divine transcendence. In this case, the response was even given in identical words.[7]

There are therefore three important affirmations in Charles Wesley's poems that run counter to the expectations we might have of a devotion shaped by its context in the early modern period of Enlightenment. First, created being was contingent, not autonomous. Second, human and created being possessed an inherent entelechy, oriented, that is, toward final causes beyond itself, destined as it was for a divine end. And, third, divine being was yet infinite, far surpassing comparison to created being and beyond the power of human telling. As Charles Wesley wrote elsewhere in adoration of the Holy Trinity:

Beyond our utmost thought,
And reason's proudest flight,
We comprehend Him not,
Nor grasp the Infinite,
But worship in the Mystic Three
One God to all eternity.[8]

> *Charles Wesley was not directly entering into late medieval debates about universals or analogy of being, but nevertheless the language of worship and devotion that he employed did a kind of metaphysical work that was above its intellectual pay grade.*

Jason Vickers makes the important point that Charles Wesley approached the mystery of the Godhead not by way of speculation but of ontological affirmation in worship. Early in the eighteenth century, fierce theological battles were fought between the orthodox party in the Church of England and the Deists over the nature of God, in which the orthodox sought to provide a rational account of personhood in God that would not entail a belief in three distinct gods. In this debate, the orthodox apologists won the battle but lost the war, as theology became sterile in losing touch with is sources in doxology. Or, as Vickers puts it in contemporary terms, all the focus was upon providing a rational defense of the immanent Trinity, without reference to the economic Trinity. Vickers writes, "Charles' doctrine of the Trinity is primarily, if not exclusively, concerned with the divine economy, i.e. with the Holy Spirit's coming to dwell in us so that we might become 'partakers of the divine nature', and not with demonstrating that a doctrine of the immanent Trinity was compatible with or confirmable by unaided human reason."[9] I think something similar could be said about how Wesley approached the mystery of creation itself as sustained by the life of God. He approached this cosmological mystery by way of doxology.

In his hymns Charles Wesley was not directly entering into late medieval debates about universals or analogy of being, but nevertheless the language of worship and devotion that he employed did a kind of metaphysical work that was above its intellectual pay grade, so to speak. Charles Wesley, like his brother, admired Isaac Newton's natural philosophy and John Locke's empirical epistemology, as also much of the physico-theology of the period, and he shared in and rejoiced in what some have called the moderate Enlightenment, marveling at the order of the natural world revealed by experimental science and mathematics as confirmation of the truths of revelation. Both Wesleys believed, however, that divine revelation went far beyond what natural reason could infer from natural phenomena. After natural philosophy had explained so much with respect to terrestrial and interstellar physics, along with the workings and classification of biological life, what remained? John Wesley wrote, "What remains of Natural Philosophy, is The Doctrine concerning God and Spirits. But, in the tracing of this, we can neither depend upon Reason nor Experiment. Whatsoever Men know, or can know concerning them, must be drawn from the Oracles of God. Here, therefore, we are to look for no new Improvements, but to *stand in the good old Paths:* To content ourselves with what God has been pleased to reveal; with *the faith once delivered to the saints.*"[10] While there was never any question of a Hobbesian materialism or freethinking Deism shaping the outlook of early evangelical leaders such as the Wesleys, there may have been a danger as the century progressed to see more and more phenomena as simply natural. Here, though, is where the language of devotion shaped a metaphysical outlook a priori.

Reg Ward described the ways in which something similar happened for continental Pietists. John Wesley published one of Gerhard Tersteegen's hymns that began, "Lo, God is here! Let us adore, / And own how dreadful is this place!" This simple invocation of God's presence did metaphysical work. As Ward says with characteristic terseness, "It perfectly encapsulates Tersteegen's reply to both the early Enlightenment which seemed to be exiling God from his universe, and the physico-theologians who could only bring Him back at the end of a long argument."[11] A simple hymn seems to punch above its weight intellectually. It is like the devout poet George Herbert praying (in what is now a hymn), "Teach me, my God and King, in all things thee to see." The pure in heart do not simply see God; they see God in everything. This was how it was for Ignatius Loyola at the end of his life. Likewise, Julian of Norwich's simple vision of the world as an object the size of a hazelnut held in God's hand, whose very being was sustained only because God was its Maker, Keeper, and Lover, was as well

an eloquent ontology, and she expressed the same sense of a suspended universe as Charles Wesley did under the image of the planets and stars "depending" in golden chains from the Spirit. Piety had metaphysical implications for all these Christian people in different times and places.

We should remind ourselves that throughout the poem, "Author of Every Work Divine," Charles Wesley does not simply describe the Spirit's work, but he addresses the Spirit personally in an encomium of praise. Like the philosophical work that Augustine did in Book X of the *Confessions*, the metaphysical affirmations that Charles Wesley made were made in the form of prayer in a direct address to the third person of the Trinity. Just as Augustine looked around at all he could see, and everything seemed to speak to him, announcing its own contingency, saying, "We did not make ourselves, but he who abides forever made us," so also the prayerful disposition of the Charles Wesley, hymning the Holy Spirit, does the same.

Thus, it is in the consciousness of the saint, who offers praise to God, that the creation finds its fulfillment. Jonathan

Edwards would call this the consent of being to Being that is excellency or beauty itself. The metaphysic that Edwards worked out in his philosophy, like the picture of the world suggested in the poetry of Charles Wesley, was in the end one of wonder, love, and praise.

The Museum of the History of Science in Oxford is on Broad Street around the corner from Hertford College where Jim Houston was a fellow before coming to be the founding principal of Regent College. On the main staircase is a monumental picture of the moon that from a distance and on first appearance could be taken for a photograph from NASA. It is, in fact, a detailed pastel by John Russell (1745–1806), a younger contemporary of Charles Wesley and an outspoken evangelical. He was the leading pastelist of the period and a member of the Royal Academy. Russell was also a friend of the Sir William Herschel and an avid amateur philosopher whose studies of the moon for a twenty-year period are held now at the museum in Oxford. Among these studies are some wonderful details visible only upon inspection up close. He has embedded angels with delicate feathered wings among the craters and crevices on the moon's service. At the height of the Enlightenment and in the midst of the Scientific Revolution, this evangelical astronomer still could not help himself. The world was just too charged with the grandeur of God. Russell's God, like that of Charles Wesley, was the God of nature and of grace. ✗

Notes

1. The original hymnbook is John and Charles Wesley, *Hymns of Petition and Thanksgiving for the Promise of Father* (Bristol, 1746). It is available at the webpage for Charles Wesley's Published Verse at the Center for Studies in the Wesleyan Tradition, Duke Divinity School: http://www.divinity.duke.edu/initiatives-centers/cswt/wesley-texts/charles-wesley.

2. W.R. Ward, *Early Evangelicalism: A Global Intellectual History, 1670–1789* (Cambridge: Cambridge University Press, 2006), 11.

3. Alexander Pope, *Essay on Man* (London, 1763), 24.

4. John and Charles Wesley, *Hymns and Sacred Poems* (London, 1739), 184–85. For the modern edition, see John Wesley, *A Collection of Hymns for the Use of the People Called Methodists*, ed. Franz Hildebrandt and Oliver A. Beckerlegge, vol. 7 of the *Bicentennial Edition of the Works of John Wesley* (Nashville: Abingdon, 1983), hymn 363, p. 532. The hymn is titled "Hymn to the Holy Ghost."

5. John Wesley, *A Survey of the Wisdom of God in the Creation, or, A Compendium of Natural Philosophy* (Bristol, 1763), 1:iv (emphasis his).

6. Ibid., iii (emphasis his).

7. The way in which Wesley could survey experimental science and still see all of it as a matter only of instrumental causes and not an explanation of material or final causes is illustrated in his conclusion to chap. 1 on the human body: "With what holy fear should we *pass the time of our sojourning here* below.... Trusting for continual Preservation, not merely on our own Care, but on the Almighty Hand, which formed the admirable Machine, directs its Agency and supports its Being." The body could thus be described in the terms of the regnant mechanical science as a machine, but form, purpose, being, and agency are all alike referred to God and therefore call for an attitude of faith. Wesley, *Survey*, 1:70 (emphasis his).

8. Charles Wesley, *Hymns on the Trinity* (Bristol, 1767), Hymn 41, p. 123–24.

9. Jason E. Vickers, "Charles Wesley and the Revival of the Doctrine of the Trinity: A Methodist Contribution to Modern Theology," in *Charles Wesley: Life, Literature and Legacy*, ed. Kenneth C. Newport and Ted A. Campbell (Peterborough: Epworth, 2007), 288.

10. Wesley, *Survey*, 14–15 (emphasis his).

11. Ward, *Early Evangelicalism*, 59.

The Transformation of Simon Peter

Markus Bockmuehl

Markus Bockmuehl is Professor of Biblical and Early Christian Studies and Fellow in Theology at Keble College, Oxford.

My subject is a spiritual mentor and joyful pastor to a people in exile, one who unites in his person the roles of Christian visionary and teacher of the treasury of tradition. Born in the far North, he first made his mark in the public role he held in the bracing and invigorating intellectual capital of the South. By far his greatest and most lasting achievement, however, took shape in a second career that left contemporaries at home wondering what had become of him: he brought his increasingly international work to a point in laying the foundation of a great spiritual project in the far West, an edifice whose influence for good and for God reached out to every corner of the globe.

Much of this is also patently true of James M. Houston, who over nearly four decades has been just such a mentor, friend, and pastor to me and my family. Like the visionary architect inducting his engineers ankle-deep in the mud of his construction site, during the early days of Regent College Houston invited my father Klaus and others to gaze with him in anticipation on a palace of Christian formation where bystanders could only see two shabby fraternity huts beginning to spill over into an unbecoming portable unit in the parking lot. (Sooner than either man expected, Jim's joyful brand of shepherding the exiles helped their initially formal relationship to blossom into a close spiritual friendship, as Jim accompanied my father in his long journey to the city of God with daily visits to his bedside.) It was in those frat houses that in the early 1980s he instilled in me and my contemporaries the aspiration and desire for a Christian mind nourished on far richer spiritual fare than was on offer in the cafeteria of contemporary church life we had previously known. Before long, the mentor once again saw things I could not see and, much against my own better instincts and stated intentions, talked me into the pursuit of a doctorate! Jim has continued in the decades since to accompany my journey with a fatherly interest and care. I offer him this essay as a small public token of a lifelong filial gratitude.

My subject here, however, is not Jim Houston but another exile—Simon Peter.[1] Why did this mysterious apostle, about whom so little is known from the New Testament, nevertheless take on such enormous significance in the later life of the church? Part of the answer to that complex question undoubtedly lies in the extent to which, ever since the earliest years of the church, he has seemed to exemplify something of the heart of Christian discipleship. The figure of Peter somehow embodies both its frail complexity and its dynamic grace of transformation, from heights of buoyant success into the abyss of abject failure, and yet onward to a joyful peace and a purified hope.

I propose here to foreground this exemplary aspect of Peter's discipleship by gradually closing in from its general appearance to its twin foci of testing and faithfulness. To that end we will begin with half a dozen "big questions" about Peter

CRUX: Fall 2012/Vol. 48, No. 3

before zeroing in on one particular text from the passion narrative and pairing it with a fascinating second-century tradition about the apostle's martyrdom.

The Vocation of Simon Peter: Six Big Questions

1. Who Was He?

The short answer of who was Peter will be familiar to most readers. Simon Peter, Son of Jonah, was a Galilean Jewish fisherman from Bethsaida who moved to Capernaum perhaps in conjunction with his marriage. He became one of the twelve close disciples of Jesus, indeed the one singled out as their leader and spokesman. He was highly enthusiastic about recognizing Jesus as Messiah. But like all Jews of his day, including Jesus's closest disciples and, for that matter, Saul of Tarsus, Peter did not think this was compatible with the idea of his violent death, and certainly not by crucifixion. After denying Jesus and fleeing on the night of his arrest, Peter was confronted and commissioned by the risen Jesus and became the leading missionary of the newly minted Jerusalem church to Jewish believers—from Judaea to Antioch, Northern Asia Minor, Greece, and Rome, where he died as a martyr under Nero. The New Testament credits Peter with two letters, and second-century Christians transmitted a large number of traditions and legends associated with his name.

It would doubtless be worthwhile to probe and question this thumbnail profile at much greater length; and in other contexts I have myself done so.[2] Here, I wish to pursue a handful of less familiar aspects of Peter's life and identity, and then use those to help gain some leverage of understanding as we turn to the passion text in the second half of this essay.

2. What Do His Four Names Tell Us?

The New Testament, confusingly, knows Peter by four different names—one Greek and three Hebrew or Aramaic: Simon or Simeon; Peter (*Petros*); Bar Yona, or Son of Jonah; and Cephas (*Kefa*).

Simeon is the name of an Israelite patriarch and one of the Twelve Tribes. The name had disappeared for many centuries and returned to popularity only about two hundred years earlier, apparently in connection with a rise in Jewish hopes for national restoration (a custom that also, for example, remains widespread among Israeli families today). This resonance might still have been understood around the time of Peter's birth in the late first century BC, and the choice of name may hint that his parents shared in such Jewish aspiration.

Yonah, the name of Peter's father, is shared with the Old Testament prophet Jonah but otherwise appears only rarely; it may have been a particularly Galilean name.

Although Cephas means "rock," to our knowledge it was not in fact used as a name by Jews or even Christians in late antiquity. This means, conversely, that the Aramaic-speaking churches of first-century Judaea seized on this unique name as the one that most clearly distinguished Peter. And this may also be why Paul retains this as his own preferred usage: he almost always calls Peter Cephas, perhaps ever since he first made his acquaintance in Jerusalem (Gal. 1:18; 2:11; the only exception is Gal. 2:7–8).

So what about the name Peter? Although relatively rare, it is in fact attested as a name in ancient Jewish sources. My view is that the apostle's unusual background in Bethsaida, with a brother and a close friend known only by strongly Hellenized names (Andrew, Philip), means that he probably knew tolerable Greek from childhood and may well have had the *Greek* nickname *Petros* ("stone" or "pebble") from the start. If so, then it was Jesus who applied to him the *Aramaic* translation *Kefa* as a name, interpreting his Greek name in Jewish terms of "the Rock": your name is *Petros*, you will in fact be *Kefa*, the Rock on which I will build my church. Wordplay on the Greek word *petra* ("rock") is also found in Jewish sources to identify a faithful person like Abraham on whom God builds the foundation of his people.

3. What Difference Did Bethsaida Make?

John 1:44 is the only place in the New Testament which tells us that Peter and his brother Andrew came from the village of Bethsaida on the Sea of Galilee. Recent excavations have shown it to be a small town of pretty humble architecture and modest material culture. Surprisingly, archaeologists have found no indication of any substantial Jewish presence or religious observance. Its culture in the first century was under strongly Hellenistic and Greek-speaking influence. If there were any Jews there, then unlike in other towns in the area they seem to have left no signs of a way of life that distinguished them culturally or linguistically from their Gentile neighbours.[3]

That high degree of accommodation or assimilation is also reflected in the names of Jesus's disciples Peter, Andrew, and Philip, all of whom the Fourth Gospel identifies as coming from the same village of Bethsaida (John 1:44; 12:21), whose Hellenizing heritage is apparent in several gospel stories. These three are the only ones among the Twelve whose primary names are Greek. In John 12:20–22, Philip and Andrew are the contact point for the Greeks who want to see Jesus, and in John 6:5, Jesus turns unhesitatingly to Philip for local knowledge of the area before the feeding of the multitude.

Jewish culture and religion were generally more marginal here in the lands of the former Northern tribes, long since settled predominantly by Gentiles. Even in Galilee, West of the Jordan, the majority Jewish population was to a significant extent due to a deliberate recolonization policy implemented by the temporarily independent Maccabean state less than two centuries earlier. To the Judaean establishment, Galilean Jews appeared just as uncouth and unwashed as "colonials" of any other age might seem to those in the perceived centre: culturally boorish, religiously suspect, and mocked for their accent—a prejudice Peter encounters when he is challenged at the trial of Jesus "the Galilean" in the house of Caiaphas (Matt. 26:73; cf. v. 69).

Peter thus probably grew up fully bilingual in a Jewish minority setting. That his family and their friends were at ease with their Greek-speaking environment seems in any case reflected in the names they gave to their children—interestingly Peter is the only one of the Bethsaida trio whose Jewish name (Simon, i.e., Simeon) we know. Philip the Tetrarch, the local potentate, liked the place and visited periodically, until a couple of years after Jesus's ministry he decreed that the village should be turned into a proper Hellenistic city called Julias—though he died before the work progressed very far. It is certainly interesting that Luke and John refer to Bethsaida as a city (Luke 9:10; John 1:44), while Mark reflects the earlier usage during Jesus's ministry in describing it as a village (8:23, 26). Understandably, given Philip's pro-Roman politics, there were considerable sympathies for the pagan imperial cult, including apparently even a small temple to Julia Livia.

Bethsaida's rejection of Jesus is a notable sore point in the gospels. Matthew, Mark, and Luke mention the village only five times, but nowhere do they give us the slightest hint that Peter came from there or had any dealings with it. Based only on the Synoptic Gospels, we would have guessed that Peter had always lived in Capernaum. It is there that we find "the house of Simon and Andrew"; and there he lives together with his wife and her mother.[4] Only John tells us about Bethsaida's connection with any of Jesus's disciples. According to Matthew and Luke it was a place where, along with Chorazin, Jesus performed "mighty deeds" (Luke 10:13 par. Matt 11:21). But both villages had failed to respond to Jesus's ministry, and he formally condemns them:

> Woe to you, Chorazin! Woe to you, Bethsaida! For if the deeds of power done in you had been done in Tyre and Sidon, they would have repented long ago, sitting in sackcloth and ashes. But at the

judgment it will be more tolerable for Tyre and Sidon than for you. (Luke 10:13–14)[5]

Given the claims here, it is striking that the evangelists tell us virtually nothing about these supposed "deeds of power" at Bethsaida. Matthew in particular, despite his keen interest in Peter, virtually eliminates Bethsaida: his one reference to it comes in this harsh word of judgement. It is possible that even in the evangelist's day it continued to prove particularly resistant to the gospel mission.[6] A similar disappointment may speak in a Jewish Christian annotation preserved in the church fathers, which claims that Jesus performed no less than fifty-three miracles at Bethsaida and Chorazin.[7]

So it seems that the New Testament gospel tradition may be engaging in a kind of conspiracy of silence. We find that the canonical gospels locate only *two* miracles near Bethsaida, neither of them based in the village itself: the feeding of the multitude somewhere in the vicinity of Bethsaida in Luke 9[8] and the unusual two-stage healing in Mark 8 of the blind man who first sees "people walking like trees" (vv. 8:22–26).

Whatever their Bethsaida background may have been, at some stage Peter and his brother moved to the more clearly Jewish environment of Capernaum and made contact with the national renewal movements of John the Baptist and Jesus. There is a remarkably twenty-first-century ring about the idea that growing up in an embattled minority context can force you either to translate and sublimate or

> *Peter's upbringing outside the Galilean heartland left him culturally better equipped than many of his fellow disciples to integrate that vision of the gospel in his future ministry from Jerusalem to Antioch and Rome.*

else to intensify and radicalize your tribal convictions.

What did this mean for Peter? His background in Bethsaida certainly taught him how to survive in a minority situation. Like Saul of Tarsus, he might become either a militant Jewish nationalist concerned with the ethnic restoration of Israel or alternatively fully engaged in articulate converse with the Gentile world. There may certainly be hints of nationalist zeal not least in narratives of Caesarea Philippi or of the conflict at Gethsemane. Yet one way or another, we also know that Peter did come to be persuaded of the gospel's outreach to both Jews and Gentiles. His upbringing outside the Galilean heartland left him culturally better equipped than many of his fellow disciples to integrate that vision of the gospel in his future ministry from Jerusalem to Antioch and Rome.

4. Did Fishing Have a Lasting Impact?

Does Peter's background yield anything more for our understanding of the man he became, the reasons for his move to Capernaum, or how his fishing career in Galilee relates to his career as a fisher of people? The church fathers consistently assumed that Peter came from exceedingly humble circumstances, that in his youth he was very poor and perhaps even orphaned.[9] By the time we encounter him in the gospel call narrative, it is true that as a fisherman near Capernaum he enjoyed somewhat greater socio-economic security than Galilean day labourers or tenant farmers for absentee landlords, who suffered the constant threat of unemployment and typically struggled along at a precarious subsistence level. That said, Peter was evidently not as well off as certain other disciples—notably the family of Zebedee who had their own boat and hired staff (Mark 1:19–20). In terms of his education, the Jerusalem authorities in Acts 4:13 evidently regard Peter as an uneducated, common man. We cannot assume he had anything more than a basic Jewish family upbringing.

More specifically, the gospels give us some intriguing insights into Peter's connection with the northern coastline of the Sea of Galilee near Bethsaida. In their call narrative, Mark and Matthew show Peter and Andrew engaged in cast-net fishing—throwing their circular nets from the shore or while standing in shallow waters (Matt. 4:18 par. Mark 1:16). Only one single passage in Luke implies that Peter may have owned or even had the use of a boat (Luke 5:3). The story of Mark and Matthew gives the impression that Jesus walks along the shore and finds Simon and Andrew standing and casting their nets "into the sea" (Mark 1:16) from there. Until the beginning of the twentieth century, indeed, the deployment of the circular cast-nets often had Palestinian fishermen standing on the shore or in the shallows of the lake. Whether on the shore or from boats, they would take advantage of the large shoals of indigenous fish (*musht*, today sold as "St. Peter fish") that in the winter months congregate around the northern part of the lake. Favourite locations were Capernaum's fishing outpost of Tabgha with its warm springs on the lakebed, and also the mouth of the Jordan near Bethsaida. It is there that fish entered or left the lake, and so they were often sufficiently plentiful to catch without using a boat.

All this does not of course limit this call narrative to a particular time and location; in fact Luke has quite a different version, in which Jesus seems already to have a prior relationship with Peter (see 4:38–39 preceding 5:1–11). But the distinctive use of the cast-net does make excellent sense on the shoreline around Capernaum and Bethsaida, and lends a particular vibrancy to the fishing metaphors used in connection with Jesus's teaching on discipleship.

The name of Peter's hometown of Bethsaida itself means "place of fishing." Even after its decline in the third century, the rabbis long remembered the locale precisely for the rich variety of its fish.[10] The gospels of course deploy plenty of stories, miracles, and teachings about different kinds of fish, fishermen,[11] fishing nets,[12] the fishing "catch,"[13] and so on. Mary Magdalene comes from Magdala, home to a thriving industry of pickling fish for export.

Most famously, perhaps, Jesus calls Peter and Andrew to become men who "fish for people."[14] This is an eschatologically charged assignment that evokes Jeremiah's prophecy about the final ingathering of Israel: "I will bring them back to their own land that I gave to their ancestors. I am now sending for many fishermen, says the Lord, and they shall catch them" (16:15–16).

Such fishing images turn out to be not just incidental but integral to the very fabric of Peter's apostolic role. The book of Acts offers tantalizing hints of the extent to which these metaphors continue to evoke Peter's past as a fisherman in understanding the future missionary. In a kind of flashback to Bethsaida, Peter in Acts 10 had an eye-opening vision at Jaffa in which he saw lowered from heaven in a fishing boat's sail[15] the sort of indiscriminate commingling of clean and unclean fish and animals that was indeed the diet of his neighbours at Bethsaida. In light of this, he understands God's gospel as reaching out to all nations; and thus he is encouraged to set out into the deep unknown and put down his net for a catch.

5. What Ever Became of Peter in the End?

Given how consistently important Peter seems to be among the disciples and in the gospel narrative, it is certainly striking how silent the rest of the New Testament is about what happened to him. The book of Acts presents itself in its opening verses as the Acts of the risen and ascended Jesus; and the two chief human protagonists within it are clearly Peter in chapters 1–12 and Paul in 13–28, who engage in parallel missions involving preaching to Jews and to Gentiles, miracles, as well as persecution. So it seems an extraordinary fact that Acts makes no reference to the deaths of either Peter or Paul, and does not even place Peter anywhere near Rome—despite the fact that its narrative ends in Rome and it may even have been written there in the last couple of decades of the first century.

The last we hear of Peter is that he is imprisoned by an opportunistic Herod Agrippa I at Passover in the year 41 or 42 and then miraculously escapes—after which Luke simply adds, perhaps with a nod and a wink, "he went to another place"—leaving us to wonder, rather like his prison guards, "what had become of Peter" (12:17–18). Peter does resurface for a brief cameo appearance at the apostolic council held in Jerusalem seven years later (Acts 15), but that is the last we hear of him in Acts.

Aside from Acts relating Peter's stay in places like Lydda, Joppa, and Caesarea on the coast, the letters of Paul and Peter suggest he also went further afield to Antioch, Corinth, and perhaps even as far as the Black Sea. Nowhere does the New Testament unambiguously mention his presence in Rome, although there may well be an allusion to this at the end of 1 Peter (5:13). Although 1 Corinthians knows about Peter as a missionary traveling with his wife, it is intriguing that Romans, written by Paul to Rome around the year 57, makes no mention of Peter (though some detect a diplomatic allusion in 15:20).

For these and other reasons, some scholars have argued quite seriously that all the evidence suggests that Peter never left Palestine but died in his bed in Jerusalem around the year 55. But in fact the evidence for Peter's ministry and martyrdom is both diverse and widespread; it includes well over a dozen Christian literary sources from the first and second centuries, and the dramatic twentieth-century archaeological discoveries of a mid-second-century

> *Jesus calls Peter and Andrew to become men who "fish for people." This is an eschatologically charged assignment that evokes Jeremiah's prophecy about the final ingathering of Israel.*

memorial on the Vatican hill. There are even occasional corroborating hints in pagan sources like Tacitus and others. No Jewish or pagan critic of Christianity ever disputes the claim that Peter was crucified in Rome under Nero. Just as significantly, no other Christian site was ever claimed to be Peter's tomb.

6. Why Does Peter Matter?

And why should any of this matter? After all, it seems to make no difference to any major Christian beliefs in Scripture or the Creeds.

In spite of that, I want to suggest that Peter's life and death actually matter a great deal. It is in fact on the faithfulness of this memory of Peter that a good deal of subsequent Christian identity ultimately rides. If the twin apostolic pillars Peter and Paul were indeed martyred in Rome within a relatively short time of each other, then their uncontradicted adoption as exemplary twin witnesses by the Christian community of that place inevitably weakens the explanatory power of theories that try to explain the New Testament church as irreconcilably divided from the start between Peter and Paul, between communities of Jewish and others of Gentile believers in Jesus.

Such views certainly have an ancient and venerable pedigree; they were famously advocated as early as the second century by Marcion of Sinope (d. ca. 160), a powerful interpreter of Paul and temporary resident of Rome. And they may help to shine a probing critical searchlight on some interesting silences and puzzles of the New Testament sources about Peter. But the idea that Peter ended his life literally and metaphorically two thousand kilometres from Rome or indeed from Paul, finds no known support, whether friendly or hostile, during the period when Christian writers could still legitimately appeal to the memory of the apostolic generation or of their students.

Throughout the later first and second centuries there is in fact a continuity of living memory that attests Peter's death in Rome, both in the East and in the West. He was remembered as the leading apostolic witness of Jesus, who, like Paul, came to Rome to advance the gospel and gave his ultimate testimony there. In that sense he went on to live out his unique ministry of responsible under-shepherd for the Good Shepherd who entrusts him with the care of his sheep (John 21:15–17). On that history hangs not perhaps the truth of Jesus and his gospel, but certainly the truth of his church as the bearer of that gospel. It is this that grounds its link with the apostolic witness—and thus with what the New Testament claims is "the faith that was once for all entrusted to the saints" (Jude 3).

The Transformation of Simon Peter: Second-Chance Discipleship

Talking the Talk: Peter at Gethsemane

Peter's transformation from backwoods fisherman to global fisher for people certainly makes for an engaging story. But there is one additional human element of the story that has persistently intrigued readers of the gospels, and which accounts for this apostle's peculiar and lasting power to exemplify and inspire Christian discipleship since antiquity. It is the profoundly transformative sense of a fallible and imperfect character given grace to make good on his failings: the work of Christ in his life is seen to empower this well-intentioned but rough-hewn and flawed disciple to do the right thing at the second time of asking.

The argument famously takes its point of departure immediately following the last supper.

> When they had sung a hymn, they went out to the Mount of Olives. Then Jesus said to them, "You will all become deserters because of me this night; for it is written, 'I will strike the shepherd, and the sheep of the flock will be scattered.' But after I am raised up, I will go ahead of you to Galilee." Peter said to him, "Though all become deserters because of you, I will never desert you." Jesus said to him, "Truly I tell you, this very night, before the cock crows, you will deny me three times." Peter said to him, "Even though I must die with you, I will not deny you." And so said all the disciples. (Matt 26:30–35)

All four gospels depict Peter as the first among disciples, time and again singled out as the spokesman and leader among the Twelve. Although quick and enthusiastic to follow Jesus and affirm him as God's chosen Messiah, he is at the same time slow and strongly resistant to the idea that this Messiah might be called to die sacrificially for Israel by surrendering his life into the hand of God's enemies. The Peter of the gospels is committed but lacks discretion and staying power. He is courageous but easily thrown by things he cannot accept, and may then resist them forcefully.

This already happens to him at Caesarea Philippi: when Jesus asks his disciples in Matthew 16, "Who do you say that I am?" Peter makes the first clear confession of Jesus as Messiah and Son of the living God (16:15). Jesus praises him for voicing this insight revealed to him by God, and in Matthew identifies Peter the Rock as the one on whom he will build his church. But as soon as Jesus goes on to elaborate that God has sent him as a Messiah who will lay down his life for God's people, Peter immediately objects strongly and rejects Jesus's interpretation out of hand. That is not what he meant at all! As a result Jesus rebukes him as harshly and forcefully as if he were the mouthpiece of Satan.

Clearly that story paints a picture of mixed emotions for Peter, as within the

> *Throughout the later first and second centuries there is in fact a continuity of living memory that attests Peter's death in Rome, both in the East and in the West.*

space of two or three sentences Jesus follows an affirmation of the highest praise with a volley of ferocious condemnation.

In Gethsemane, at the point where Jesus is about to give up his life, Peter resists once again. He refuses out of hand the idea that Jesus might die without resistance and alone, that the disciples will simply abandon him in his hour of need. He speaks for the disciples in this respect, but is determined to outdo them all: "Though all become deserters because of you, I will never desert you. … Even though I must die with you, I will not deny you."

Peter may be the disciple who most strikingly and encouragingly exemplifies Christian discipleship for those who may not always get things right the first time around.

Dying with Jesus as such appears not to trouble Peter. What he cannot accept is the Messiah who dies without a fight, and the prediction of his own failure. And indeed he is depicted in all the gospels as sticking with Jesus longer than any of the Twelve—though it is unclear whether he is more foolhardy in pulling his sword at Jesus's arrest, or in then having the chutzpah of following him all the way into the High Priest's compound. Yet when it comes to the crunch at the house of Caiaphas, where Peter is challenged to identify with Jesus, he crumbles just as Jesus predicted: three times he flatly denies knowing Jesus, and when the cock crows as predicted he turns and runs away. Narratively and morally, it is the point of abject failure and darkest despair, and it was understood to be such by ancient Christian artists and hymnodists who developed this scene into a powerful parable of sin, repentance, and redemption.

Walking the Walk: The Second Chance

It is a well-known commonplace, heard from Protestant pulpits as much as from Catholic propagandists, that the New Testament Peter appears as a forgiven sinner, denying his Lord but rehabilitated and charged with a new mission. After three denials of Jesus, in John three times he answers the resurrected Jesus's question "Do you love me?" and three times his "Yes" receives Jesus's response that he is to tend the flock of Jesus.

But did Peter in fact take that second chance? Do we know if he did get it right the second time around and stood by the promise he made at Gethsemane? The New Testament only hints at an answer to that question, as we saw earlier: Acts is eloquently silent about what happened to Peter. Even the quasi-testamentary letter known as 2 Peter only hints at the apostle's impending martyrdom, recalling the importance of Petrine eyewitness testimony of Jesus's transfiguration but making very little of any element of "second-chance" faithfulness.

Precisely that element, however, surfaces with a poignant explicitness in second-century Christian memory of Peter's death in Rome. The apostle here has become the flawed but forgiven and restored disciple whose life is an encouragement to other believers. Some time around the middle decades of the second century there emerged an account of Peter's final contest with the church's enemies in Rome, culminating in his death at the hands of Nero. Anticipated around AD 100 in texts like *1 Clement*, the *Ascension of Isaiah,* and Ignatius's letter to Rome, this theme comes to narrative development in a complex of stories later known as the *Acts of Peter* (which date back to the second century but did not achieve final form until the fourth century or later). Parts of that narrative complex are clearly fanciful and legendary; though not everything necessarily falls into that category. Comparison with other sources highlights some touchingly human reflections on the ways in which Peter's martyrdom was remembered by the church.

In chapter 7 of that document, Peter encourages the church in Rome by confessing that he denied Jesus three times, but that Jesus had compassion on him. He

CRUX: Fall 2012/Vol. 48, No. 3

encourages his fellow Christians to be loyal in the face of opposition, to stand fast and not to doubt.

By the time we reach chapter 35, it has become clear that Peter's life is in danger, and the Christians of Rome entreat Peter to leave the city in order to be able to continue the Lord's work. There follows a famous description of what happens to him on his escape through the city gates onto the Appian Way:

> But Peter said to them, "Shall we act like deserters, brothers and sisters?" But they said to him, "No, it is so that you can go on serving the Lord." So he was persuaded; he departed alone and said, "Let none of you leave with me, but I will leave alone in disguise." And as he went out of the gate he saw the Lord entering Rome; and when he saw him he said, "Lord, where are you going?" And the Lord said to him, "I am going to Rome to be crucified." And Peter said to him, "Lord, are you being crucified again?" He said to him, "Yes, Peter, I am being crucified again." And when Peter came to himself and saw the Lord ascending into heaven, he turned back to Rome, rejoicing and praising the Lord because he had said, "I am being crucified." For this was about to happen to Peter. (*Acts of Peter* 35)

When the church persuades Peter to flee from Rome in disguise, he baulks at this and objects that this would be to act like a deserter—a role he evidently does not want to play again. But in the end he listens to the community and takes their advice, until his visionary encounter with Jesus on his way to crucifixion tells him dramatically where he is meant to be: with Jesus, who suffers with and through his people. So Peter turns back—a change of course that represents a spiritual conversion as much as it is a physical U-turn. The denial of the night in which Jesus died has now become the good confession. Third-century Christian artists liked to capture this point by depicting Peter together with an oversized crowing rooster on a pillar: as the rooster heralds the dawn of a new day just when the night is at its darkest, so this image of Peter juxtaposes the moment of his greatest failure with the foreshadowing of the resurrection and the powerful grace of his restoration.

The third-century church father Clement of Alexandria cites a tradition from a different but possibly related story cycle: as Peter was being taken out for crucifixion, he saw his wife being led out to her death and called out to her, "My dear, Remember the Lord!"[16]

According to the Acts of Peter the apostle is then crucified, like Jesus but upside down, in the gardens of Nero. It is a matter of historical record that since at least the mid-second century the church marked the memory of his burial on the adjacent Vatican Hill—a spot that was excavated in the twentieth century and which can be visited today.

What follows from all this for the exemplary role of Peter in early Christian memory? Peter may be the disciple who most strikingly and encouragingly exemplifies Christian discipleship for those who may not always get things right the first time around. Peter tragically fails to keep his promise at the arrest and trial of Jesus, but he goes on to embody the dramatic gospel grace of second chances. Within the period of living memory, when there were still Christians in Rome who remembered the apostle or his pupils, the accounts of his martyrdom recalled that when the crunch came a second time he did not again deny or desert Jesus, but like his Lord bore testimony with his life on a Roman cross.

Peter, then, was for the early church a paradigm example of the transformative grace that is at the heart of the Christian life. He became in that sense the patron saint of second-chance discipleship. ✗

Notes

1. This essay draws on several aspects of my longer-term project on Simon Peter recently brought to completion in a volume of specialist essays (*The Remembered Peter in Ancient Reception and Modern Debate* [Tübingen: Mohr Siebeck, 2010]) and a more synthetic monograph (*Simon Peter in Scripture and Memory: The New Testament Apostle in the Early Church* [Grand Rapids: Baker Academic, 2012]). For present purposes referencing has been kept to a minimum, but readers interested in fuller scholarly documentation may wish to consult these two volumes in the first instance, along with a linked collection of primary sources at http://simonpeter.bodleian.ox.ac.uk. I am grateful for previous opportunities to "road-test" certain parts of this argument in various settings, including the Morgan Lecture in New Testament Studies at Westerly Road Church, Princeton, NJ, on 21 May 2006.

2. See n. 1.

3. Jewish settlers in the Transjordan tetrarchy of Philip (today's Golan Heights) appear to have increased considerably under his rule (*Ant.* 17.2.2 §28); indeed Philip's father, Herod the Great, had already offered hospitality to wealthy Babylonian Jewish immigrants (e.g., *Ant* 17.2.1 §24). Nearby towns showing much clearer signs of Jewish settlement than Bethsaida include Gamla and Yehudieh.

4. Mark 1:29–31; cf. Matt. 8:14–15 par. Luke 4:38, "Peter's house." Peter's wife is also mentioned in 1 Cor. 9:5.

5. All Scripture quotations are from the NRSV, unless otherwise noted.

6. Judgement on Bethsaida is clearly expressed in the Spanish recension of 5 Ezra 1:11, an early second-century Christian addition to a Jewish apocalypse preserved in Latin: "Did I not destroy Bethsaida because of you?"

7. *Gospel of the Nazarenes* frg. 27.

8. Note that while 9:10 implies the narrative may be entering the "city," by 9:12 it has clearly moved to the wilderness.

9. So Chrysostom *Hom.* 4 on Acts 2:1–2: "he of Bethsaida, the uncouth rustic"; cf. *Hom.* 2 on John 1:1; also *Ps.-Clem. Hom.* 12.6.

10. Simeon ben Gamaliel, the son of St. Paul's teacher, was reputedly offered at Bethsaida a dish made of three hundred fish (*Jerusalem Talmud, Šeqalim* 6.2, 50a). Some scholars suspect here a catch of sardines.

11. Matt. 4:18; Mark 1:16–17; Luke 5:2.

12. Matt. 4:18, 20, 21; 13:47; Mark 1:16, 18, 19; Luke 5:2, 4, 5, 6; John 21:6, 8, 11.

13. Luke 5:4, 9.

14. Mark 1:16, 17.

15. Acts 10:11; 11:5: an *othon* with "four points." The meaning "sail" is well attested in Jewish and Greek sources. Fishing boats with "four-pointed" rectangular sails appear on mosaics and coins of the period. Contemporary visitors are shown an example in a first-century Magdala floor mosaic on display at Capernaum.

16. *Strom.* 7.11.63; cf. Eusebius, *Hist. eccl.* 3.30.2.

Joshua as Sacrament:
Spiritual Interpretation in Origen

Hans Boersma

Among the many things that fill me with gratitude when I think of Jim Houston, three stand out. First, like Origen, Jim has always rejected a party spirit and wants to be known primarily by the name of Christ, as a *vir ecclesiasticus* (man of the church). Jim has taught me to focus on what is central to the Christian faith and to celebrate this with others who belong to Christ. Second, Jim has taught me to look for the real presence of Christ wherever it may be found. His focus on what Origen terms the "incarnations" of the eternal Logos—found primarily in Christ, and in and through him also in many people and places around us—has saved me from pitfalls and made me grateful for the ways in which God is present to me today. Finally, Jim's deep conviction that the Scriptures are the book of the church and are to be read spiritually and in line with the broad Christian tradition places him in Origen's trajectory, and for this, too, I am thankful. In each of these ways, Jim has been a modern-day Origen to me. It is in thankfulness to God for Jim's real presence in my personal and academic life that I dedicate this essay to him.

Introduction

Origen of Alexandria (ca. 185–ca. 251), both one of the most influential and one of the most controversial theologians of the ante-Nicene church, continues to inspire discussion and debate among exegetes of Scripture as well as dogmatic theologians. Perhaps few aspects of his legacy are as controversial as his approach to biblical interpretation, which he famously outlines in *On First Principles*, where he advocates a threefold meaning of the biblical text: the historical, the moral, and the spiritual.[1]

The objections to Origen's spiritual interpretation are well-known. Origen derives this threefold interpretation from his tripartite anthropology: the literal meaning corresponds to the body; the moral meaning to the soul; and the spiritual meaning to the spirit. Thus, a tripartite, Platonically based anthropology determines Origen's approach to Scripture. He seems to rely more on Philo and thus on Platonic philosophical categories than on Scripture itself, which means that in his exegesis, the philosophical dross covers over the pure gold of Scripture. This Philonic influence can be seen in Origen's allegorical interpretation, which far too often downplays, ignores, or denies the historical meaning of the text. History, according to this objection, disappears as a meaningful category, to be replaced with otherworldly concerns. Briefly put, the vertical displaces the horizontal.

Furthermore, by moving directly from a historical to a moral reading of Scripture, Origen's interpretation is allegedly moralistic in character. He is mainly concerned, so the argument goes, with what the text says about Christians' moral actions; as a result, the historical particularities of the text move into the background. Immediately connected to this is the observation that Origen's allegorizing makes him largely overlook the literal meaning in order to jump straight to the moral and allegorical levels of

Hans Boersma is J. I. Packer Professor of Theology at Regent College.

reading, which—seeing they are bereft of historical grounding—cannot but lapse into an arbitrary imposition of meanings. The historical and the spiritual seem separated in Origen's interpretation, with the former disappearing into oblivion and the latter taking on a capricious character.

These objections have most famously and forcefully been presented by R. P. C. Hanson in his influential 1959 study *Allegory and Event*.[2] To be sure, Hanson's position forms by no means the consensus among patristic scholars. Nine years before Hanson's book appeared, Henri de Lubac published a study of Origen's interpretation of Scripture, entitled *History and Spirit*, in which he presented a vigorous defence of the Alexandrian theologian's approach to Scripture. De Lubac's study has recently been published in English translation.[3] De Lubac's defence of Origen notwithstanding, Hanson's denunciation of the latter's approach has been tremendously influential, not in the least because it fit the more historical mould that dominated so much biblical exegesis of the twentieth century.

In this essay, I will focus on Origen's homilies on Joshua, and I hope to show from these homilies (as well as from additional reflections on Origen's theology) that, even though he does downplay the historical character of some events related to us in the book of Joshua, Origen nonetheless values the historical level in a penultimate sense as a result of the sacramental cast of his exegesis. We can only appreciate how Origen's exegesis functions if and when we come to understand the sacramental structure that lies at the basis of his interpretation.[4] What is more, inasmuch as history serves in this sacramental role, the footing of Origen's valuation of history is more secure than that of many contemporary historical exegetes, for whom the category of history has no grounding beyond itself.[5] In this essay, therefore, I hope to show something of the sacramental character of Origen's interpretation of Scripture, particularly as it comes to the fore in his homilies on Joshua.

Origen's Polemical Context

There is no denying that Origen's interpretation of Scripture is markedly different from nearly all modern and late modern readings. The very strangeness of his exegesis, the mere fact that it is so different from what we are used to, makes it difficult for us to recognize its value. I suspect that in many cases, we do not disagree with Origen from the outset. Disagreement, after all, implies understanding. One significant obstacle in our understanding of Origen's reading of Scripture is that we are so conditioned by our modern surroundings that reading Origen leads us into an alien world, a world that, at least initially, we have difficulty recognizing, let alone comprehending. And without comprehension, we cannot possibly come to agreement or disagreement—which, of course, hinders our enjoyment of Origen's exegetical work. One of our first tasks then, if we are to evaluate his allegorizing of Scripture, is to familiarize ourselves with some of his writings, and for this occasion, I have chosen to reflect on Origen's homilies on Joshua. I have purposely chosen *this* particular Bible book because it is, more than any other, a book of violence. It is a book that offends, a book that not only ancient readers but also contemporary Christians find difficult to appropriate. How is a book such as Joshua—with its stories of conquest, its incitement to genocide, and its distributions of conquered areas—how is this Christian Scripture?

This question—how we can consider the book of Joshua to be Christian Scripture—was Origen's question no less than it is ours. To be sure, as I indicated, our twenty-first-century context is rather different from Origen's third-century world. Our apprehension of violence is fuelled by late modern sensibilities that condition us to be fearful of the role that religion may play in military conflicts, nervous about the imposition of ideological regimes that do not allow for difference or dissent, and concerned with the victims of oppression, abuse, and marginalization.

24

The postmodern celebration of difference goes hand in hand with the rejection of the violent hegemony of sameness that characterized modernity. In such a context, it is difficult to appropriate Old Testament books such as Joshua.

Nonetheless, Origen, too, struggled with the appropriation of Joshua. It was particularly the opposition of two religious groups that made it difficult for Christian theologians such as Origen to refer to the book of Joshua as Christian Scripture. Two alternative interpretations vied for people's allegiance, both of which rejected a Christian reading of this Bible book. The first was a Jewish reading of the book. Throughout his homilies and commentaries, Origen finds himself at odds with Jewish readings of the text. In particular, he objects to the literalness of Jewish interpretation. Repeatedly, when he makes his case for a spiritual reading of the text, Origen polemically questions the Jewish approach. For instance, when Joshua the son of Nun is told to circumcise the Israelites a second time (Josh. 5:2), Origen immediately comments: "I may wish in this place to inquire of the Jews how anyone is able to be circumcised a second time with the circumcision of the flesh."[6] Origen here makes the simple observation that it is physically not possible to circumcise a person twice. As a result, he puts forward a spiritual reading, according to which the first circumcision is the putting aside of the errors of idolatry in favour of the law of Moses and the second is the acceptance of Christ, the circumcision by means of "the rock, who is Christ."[7] Origen speaks of "those Jewish defenders of the letter who are ignorant of the spirit of the Law."[8] He mentions the person who is "outwardly a Jew" and thinks that "nothing else but wars" constitute the topic of the book of Joshua.[9] As a result, the Jews "become cruel and implacable," maintains Origen.[10] A strictly historical reading, in Origen's context, is the reading advocated by his Jewish opponents.

Our first instinct, perhaps, is to shrink back from such anti-Jewish rhetoric as unseemly, even anti-Semitic.[11] But we need to be careful with such accusations, understandable though they may be, particularly in the light of the horrible history of the twentieth century. Without trying to excuse the excesses of some of Origen's *ad hominem* statements against the Jews, we need to keep in mind that for Origen, anti-Jewish rhetoric is less a matter of anti-Semitism than it is a matter of securing the right to interpret the Scriptures from the perspective of the reality of Christ. We cannot understand the fathers' anti-Jewish discourse if we fail to keep in mind the importance of the question, "Whose Bible is it?" with regard to the Hebrew Bible or the Old Testament. So, in Homily 17, Origen insists that in the division of the land of Judea that the book of Joshua relates, we can see a "copy and shadow" of a heavenly division (cf. Heb. 8:5).[12] Accordingly, Origen regards the earthly Jerusalem, the temple and the altar there, the visible worship with its priests and high priests, as well as the various regions and towns of Judea, as imitations of "heavenly things."[13] He observes that all these "imitations" have disappeared with the Incarnation. The reason is that "at the coming of God our Savior, truth descended from heaven."[14] And so, Origen appeals to the Jews to turn from the "shadows" and "types" to the "truth" of the reality that has come with Christ:

> If therefore, O Jew, coming to the earthly city of Jerusalem, you find it overthrown and reduced to ashes and embers, do not weep as you do now "as if with the mind of a child" [1 Cor. 14:20]; do not lament; but search for a heavenly city instead of an earthly one.

We can only appreciate how Origen's exegesis functions if and when we come to understand the sacramental structure that lies at the basis of his interpretation.

Look above! And there you will discover "the heavenly Jerusalem that is the mother of all" [Gal. 4:26].[15]

For Origen, as well as for many other church fathers, anti-Jewish rhetoric was in the first place a polemic aimed at securing the Old Testament as Christian Scripture. It had to be read not in a fleshly but in a spiritual fashion. This is not to suggest that anti-Jewish writing never slid into anti-Semitism. On a regular basis, it did. But we do need to keep in mind the hermeneutical concern—and, tied in with this, the even more important question of Christian identity—that motivated church fathers such as Origen. With twenty centuries of Christian history behind us, we have a long tradition that recognizes the Old Testament as Christian Scripture, and as a result we simply do not experience the same anxious concern as the church fathers did to secure the Old Testament as the church's book.

The second alternative Old Testament interpretation was that of the Gnostics. During much of the second and third centuries, Gnostic groups were highly influential in their attempt to supplant mainstream Christianity as the leading religion of the empire. Since Gnostics tended to be syncretistic in character and were quite willing to adopt elements of the Christian Scriptures that they could fit in with their own theological emphases, Gnosticism turned out to be a dangerous alternative to the church.[16] Many Gnostic groups aimed at secret knowledge (*gnōsis*), which would allow them to escape this evil, material world. As Walter Wink puts it, "For many Gnostics, Creation was not followed by a Fall, as in Judaism and Christianity; Creation was the Fall. They were a single, tragic event."[17] Valentinian and Basilidian Gnostics were prominent in Alexandria, while in Caesarea the Marcionites proved to be influential in their rejection of the authority of the Old Testament.[18]

Since for the fathers doctrine was always a matter of scriptural interpretation, it was primarily the reading of Scripture that divided the Christians from the Gnostics. In the late second century, St. Irenaeus had done battle with the Gnostics in his five books *Against Heresies*, and in the third century, it was up to Origen and others to fight these same heretical groups. Origen repeatedly mentions Valentinus, Basilides, and Marcion in one breath.[19] Preaching in Caesarea, he was perhaps mostly concerned with Marcion and his disciple Apelles.[20] Marcion discarded the Old Testament as unworthy of the God of the New Testament. The human ways in which the Old Testament described God (its anthropomorphisms), the violence that this God and his people embraced, and the many immoralities described in the Old Testament Scriptures led Marcion to reject the Old Testament altogether and to posit the existence of two gods: the god of the Old and the god of the New Testament. As a result, when Origen did battle with the Gnostics, this was a struggle against a literalist reading of the Old Testament, as was also his fight against Jewish interpretations.

Thus, when Joshua enlisted the Gibeonites as "hewers of wood" and "carriers of water" in the service of the Israelites (Josh. 9:21), the Marcionites objected to such an inconsiderate, perhaps even immoral, attitude on the part of Joshua. "Of course," comments Origen in Homily 10, "it must be observed that the heretics reading this passage, those who do not accept the Old Testament, are accustomed to make a malicious charge and say, 'See how Jesus the son of Nun showed no human kindness, so that, although permitting salvation, he inflicted a mark of infamy and a yoke of servitude upon those men who had come to him in supplication.'"[21] Origen then proceeds to defend Joshua's actions by contrasting the unworthy attitudes of the Gibeonites to the exemplary behaviour of Rahab, and he then provides a spiritual interpretation of the Gibeonites' identity. Gibeonites are people who go through all the right motions in church while making no effort to restrain their vices and to cultivate virtuous habits: "Let them know they will be assigned a part and lot with the Gibeonites by the Lord Jesus."[22] Origen defends Old Testament Scripture against the Gnostic accusation of cruelty by insisting on an allegorical interpretation of the text of Joshua.

Our context is in many ways different from that of Origen. But this does not render his exegesis any less timely. Origen aims his polemics against Jewish and Gnostic interpretations of Scripture. Over against the Jews, he insists that their exegesis cannot circumvent the accusation that the biblical text, with its violence and immorality, is unworthy of God. They need spiritual exegesis to overcome this difficulty. While the Gnostics do not suffer the same implication regarding religious violence, they only avoid this problem by simply rejecting the book of Joshua altogether. Both groups, however, make the same basic mistake, according to Origen: they read the text on a literal level only, and by doing so, fall into the trap of a carnal reading of the Old Testament Scriptures.[23] Both problems with which Origen struggles— that of an overly literal reading of the text and that of religious violence—are issues we today face, as well. Historical readings of Scripture, when they are solely concerned with authorial intent, are unable to overcome the postmodern accusation against the Christian faith—namely, that it has served and continues to serve as an instrument of violence. Modern exegetes who advocate a strictly literal reading of the text are faced with a stark choice: they either have to justify the violence inherent in the Old Testament or they have to abandon it as Christian Scripture. Since either option seems to me detrimental to the church, I suggest that a serious look at the third-century exegesis of Origen is well worth our while.[24]

Scripture as Incarnate Logos

For much of the Great Tradition, the term "mystery" functioned as a synonym for the word "sacrament." Susan K. Wood, in her book *Spiritual Exegesis and the Church in the Theology of Henri de Lubac*, makes the point that for de Lubac—and, we could add, for many of the fathers and medieval theologians—"the structure of allegory is fundamentally sacramental."[25] She explains this statement as follows:

> The content or signification of both the historical event and the future historical reality of Christ and the Church to which the allegorical meaning refers exceed what is observable within history. Just as what is observable within history does not limit the mystery it embodies, so too, Christian allegory is not limited to the historical dimension. That is, allegory points not only to future historical realities, but to future mysteries which, belonging to the fulfillment of history, surpass history. Thus the concept of *mysterium*, that which is hidden within, is proper to both the past historical event and the future reality it prefigures.[26]

Two comments may help clarify what it is that Wood is suggesting about spiritual interpretation. First, when allegorical exegesis insists that Old Testament events point to New Testament realities, it is not just moving from point *A* to point *B* on a chronological timeline. Allegory is not just like a prophecy-fulfillment scheme. Instead, Wood maintains, both point *A* and point *B* have a signification that exceeds or goes beyond what is observable within history.[27] Historical events are never *just* that; they are never *just* historical events. Particularly salvation-historical events always carry an extra dimension. They always point beyond history.

Second, when Old Testament events point to future events—referring to Christ or to the church—they point, says Wood, to "future mysteries." She uses the term *mysterium*. This is a sacramental term, and we would not go wrong by simply translating it as "sacrament." Sacraments are often described as visible signs of invisible realities. What sacraments do is make present God's invisible grace in our visible reality. Or, if we take our starting point in this tangible world, we could say that when created realities function as sacraments, they carry an extra, mysterious dimension; they carry a dimension that is mysterious in the sense that if one were to take all the measurements of a particular object that one possibly could—if one were to map its DNA, so to speak—he still would not fully grasp or comprehend the object. The reason is this: there's a sacramental mystery to the object, which simply isn't subject to measurement. It belongs to the invisible, eternal realm, to which we do not have access by means of the senses. Wood calls *mysterium* "that which is hidden within." We could also say it is "that which exceeds or transcends" the empirically observable.

Mysteries point from Old Testament events to New Testament realities. They do so not as if these were two unconnected events, like sign *A* pointing to reality *B*. Rather, the notion of *mysterium* or *sacramentum* means that the New Testament reality *B* already lies embedded within the original, Old Testament event *A*. Event *A* carries a mysterious presence *B* that is unobservable by the senses, but that is no less real. Event *A* carries the "real presence" of event *B*. Susan Wood's expression "future mysteries," borrowed from the Great Tradition, is paradoxical in character, since it combines horizontal, chronological connections with vertical, spiritual links. Old Testament events both point forward in time—hence the word "future"—and they point upward toward the invisible realm—hence the term "mysteries."

Diagram 1

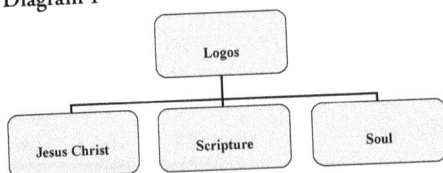

For Origen, all divine revelation functioned in thoroughly sacramental fashion. Robert J. Daly makes this clear in his foreword to an anthology of Origen's work, edited by Hans Urs von Balthasar and entitled *Spirit and Fire*. The Word, or Logos, of God, Daly explains, is central to Origen's theology. When God reveals himself in history, the eternal Logos takes on the form of earthly, temporal existence. Daly's summary of the various "incarnations" of the Logos is worth quoting in full:

> When Origen speaks of the biblical WORD, the WORD incarnate in the scriptures, at least four interconnected levels of meaning are in play. *First*, this WORD is the pre-existent, eternal, divine Logos, the Logos proclaimed in the prologue of John's gospel and expounded in extraordinary detail and depth in Origen's commentary on this prologue. *Second*, this same divine Logos is the one who took flesh of the Virgin Mary, lived and worked among us, suffered, died, rose again and ascended to the Father, where he continues to intercede for us and to work until all things have become subjected to the Father who is all in all. *Third*, this same eternal WORD who took flesh of Mary has also become incarnate in the words of scripture. *Fourth*, this same divine WORD, born of Mary and also incarnate in the scriptures, also dwells and is at work within us, espoused to our souls, calling us to make progress toward perfection, and to work with him in ascending to and subjecting all things to the Father.[28]

Daly explains that there are four levels of meaning in connection with the word "Logos." The starting-point is the eternal Logos itself, the eternal, pre-existing Son of God. This eternal Word takes on the characteristics of time and space in three different ways; or, we could also say, there are three incarnations of the eternal Word: (1) *the* Incarnation of Jesus Christ in the Virgin Mary, (2) the incarnation in the Scriptures, and (3) the incarnation in our own souls (see diagram 1).

Daly's analysis is essentially right, it seems to me—though, of course, the differences between these various "incarnations" do have to be kept in mind.[29] It is fascinating to see how for Origen the second incarnation (the Word's presence in Scripture) is intimately linked to the third (the birth of Christ in our souls). Daly adds that this final level of meaning is the "dominating" one, as it constitutes Origen's "central hermeneutical principle."[30] And, indeed, for Origen, the Logos that is present in Scripture is the same Logos that dwells also in the believer. Henri de Lubac reflects on this in his book *History and Spirit*. He makes the point that for Origen, we need to read the soul in a similar manner to the way we read Scripture. De Lubac comments: "What we call the spiritual sense in Scripture we name the image of God in the soul. And if the divine Logos is planted in each soul as he is inserted into the fabric of Scripture, are the inspired words not as engraved 'with the image of the great King' as is the human soul? It is on both sides the same impression, or rather the same Presence."[31] As we read Scripture, we come to understand ourselves in the process; and, of course, vice versa: as we come to understand ourselves better, we become more equipped to read and understand Scripture. The same Word is active both in Scripture and in ourselves, explains de Lubac.[32]

We need to briefly pause here, because de Lubac's reflection is important in connection with the fear of arbitrariness that often arises in connection with Origen's allegorical exegesis. If it is true that Scripture and the soul have the same structure—if it is true that both are, in some sense, incarnations of the eternal Logos—then Spirit-guided exegesis can hardly be arbitrary. I do not mean, of course, that the presence of the Logos in the believing soul

ensures that the believer will find just the right, objectively correct, interpretation. For Origen, there is no such thing, and neither is there such a thing for de Lubac. Rather, as de Lubac puts it, "Every time I am faithful to the Spirit of God in the interpretation of the Scriptures, my interpretation is valid in some respect."[33] Multiplicity of interpretation, on this understanding, is simply a reflection of the Spirit's plurality of gifts in the lives of believers. As long as the believer's soul reflects the "imprint" of the image of God, she will identify spiritual readings that reflect the presence of the eternal Logos.[34]

As already indicated, I believe Daly is fundamentally right in his understanding of a threefold incarnation. At the same time, his helpful discussion does need some amplification. We need to keep in mind that Origen was, as he himself calls it, a "man of the church" (*vir ecclesiasticus*): "I want to be a man of the church. I do not want to be called by the name of some founder of a heresy but by the name of Christ, and to bear that name which is called blessed on the earth. It is my desire, in deed as in Spirit, both

Diagram 2

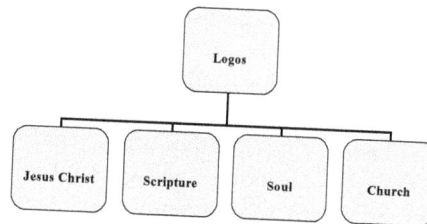

to be and to be called a Christian."[35] This beautiful passage highlights an important concern for Origen.[36] De Lubac has strongly insisted that the individual quest for God is never *just* an individual quest. It is always in *in*corporation *into* an embodiment in the body, or *corpus*, of the church.[37] So close, in fact, is the link between the church and the individual that it may be more appropriate to speak of the Word's incarnation in the church than of the Word's incarnation in the individual soul. Or, as diagram 2 makes clear, perhaps we could speak of a fourfold incarnation of the Logos: in Jesus Christ, in Scripture, in the believer, and in the church.[38]

The way in which Balthasar, in his anthology of Origen's work, structures the lengthy section on the "Word" captures this ecclesial element well. He first has a section entitled "Word with God," dealing with the eternal Logos. He then moves to a threefold incarnation: "Word as Scripture," "Word as Flesh," and "Church." As Balthasar himself puts it: "Incarnation in the scripture and in an individual body were both an image and means to the third incarnation which was the meaning and purpose of the redemption: the incarnation of the Logos in his mystical body."[39] This mystical body, the church, has existed, according to Origen, since the beginning of the world. The result is that throughout the Old Testament we see types or figures of the church. Adam and Eve's union, Noah's ark, Abraham, Jael, the bride of the Song of Songs, and the Queen of Sheba all prefigure the church of the Gentiles.[40]

The fact that the Word becomes incarnate both in Jesus Christ and in the church enables Origen to posit a close link between the two. What happens to the church happens to Christ and vice-versa, since both share in the eternal Logos.[41] Balthasar's anthology pulls together some fascinating passages from Origen's writings that illustrate this close link. Referring, for example, to opposition coming from both Jews and pagans, Origen comments:

> I see Jesus every day "giving his back to the smiters" (Isa 50:6). Go into the Jewish synagogues and see Jesus being beaten by them with blasphemous tongue. Look at the pagan assemblies, plotting against Christians and how to capture Jesus. And he "gives his back to the smiters." … So many beat and strike him, and he is silent and says not a word. … And to this day, Jesus "has not hid his face from shame and spitting" (Isa 50:6).[42]

Jesus's suffering, prophesied in Isaiah 50, continues in the church, maintains Origen. In a real sense, we could say that for Origen, the church *is* Christ, so that, along with Christ, the church is an incarnation of the eternal Logos.

De Lubac, too, draws attention to this unity between Christ and the church. In fact, he makes the daring point that the church is a "more perfect, fuller realization of the divine design" than the historical body born of the Virgin.[43] The reason for this is that the church is the reality of which the historical body of Christ was the "type" or the symbol.[44] De Lubac captures Origen's understanding of the Christ-church relationship as follows: "The historical life of Christ in his flesh and the mystical life in his Church are thus one and the same life under two different aspects, in two 'bodies', one of which is symbolic and the other symbolized."[45] For Origen, both the historical body and the ecclesial body are incarnations of the one Logos. The historical body is a prefiguration of the completion of the Logos in the eschatological, full reality of the church. In short, what we have seen so far is that the existence of multiple incarnations of one and the same Logos implies a close relationship among these various incarnate earthly realities. There is an intimate link between Scripture and the soul as well as between Christ and the church.

At the historical or horizontal level, there are, of course, all kinds of differences among these various incarnations of the Logos—differences that we can observe with the senses. Still, the close connection that we have already observed between Scripture and the soul, as well as between Christ and the church, points to the fact that if we move beyond the observable to the eternal Word itself, we come to the point (an eternal, heavenly one) where the four are not just similar, but actually identical. The multiple earthly words find their point of unity and their coherence in the eternal Word. For de Lubac, it is our purpose as believers finally to reach beyond the multiplicity of words (plural) to the simplicity of the one Word. Thus, when in the incarnate Christ we reach beyond the human nature that we observe with the senses, we arrive at his divine nature, at the eternal Word of God. Likewise, when in Scripture we go beyond the literal sense of the text to the spiritual meaning, we come to the eternal Word itself. De Lubac summarizes Origen's thought as follows:

> In his Scripture as in his earthly life, Origen thought, the Logos needs a body; the historical meaning and the spiritual meaning are, between them, like the flesh and the divinity of the Logos. All of Scripture is, so to speak, "incorporated"; like the One whom it proclaims and prepares for, it is "non in phantasia, sed in veritate" (not in fantasy, but in truth). Certainly, just as one must not stop in Christ at the man who is seen but, through the flesh that veils him to carnal eyes, perceive by faith the God who is in him, so one must go through the external history that is offered to us in the Holy Books, particularly in the Old Testament, in order to penetrate to the "spiritual mystery" that is hidden there.[46]

According to Origen, in the spiritual sense of the Bible, as in the divinity of Christ, one arrives at one and the same eternal Logos. Origen's working assumption here is that "there are not two Words any more than there are two Spirits."[47] The Word of Scripture is none other than the eternal Logos. De Lubac explains that it is "still the same word, the same biblical word, and there is no play on words in that."[48]

The obvious implication—although to my knowledge de Lubac does not spell this out—is that the soul of the individual, too, to the extent that she reaches perfection, finds her point of unity in the eternal Logos. And with regard to the church, Origen makes the same point. Not only is the body of Jesus Christ a type of the body of the church, but this connection between Christ and his church implies that the many members are eschatologically united in one body. Origen comments, for instance, that "when this resurrection of the true and perfect Body of Christ takes place ..., then his multiple members will form a single body."[49] It seems as though Origen is suggesting that the full unity of the church in the eschaton is the fullness of the eternal Logos. We may fairly suggest, then, that on the great day of the resurrection, the incarnate Christ, the Holy Scriptures, the individual soul, and the body of the church all reach their unifying apex or climax in the fullness of the eternal Word of God. Diagram 3 thus makes clear that each of the four "incarnations," as they render present the reality to which they point (understood, respectively, as Christ's divine nature, the spiritual sense of Scripture, the image of God in the soul, and the fullness of ecclesial unity), find their point of unity in the eternal Logos.

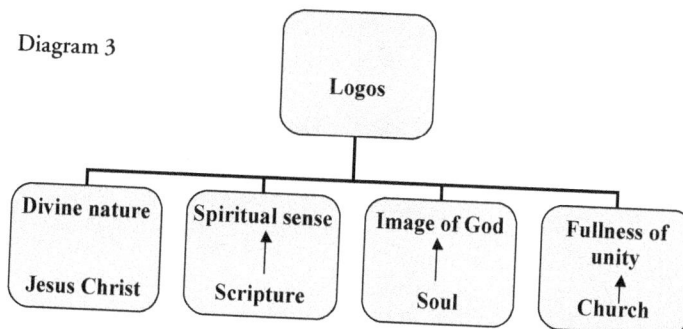

Diagram 3

Mysterii video sacramentum

So far, I have described Origen's understanding of the temporal and sensible appearances of Christ, Scripture, soul, and church as embodiments or incarnations of the eternal Logos. This is certainly true to Origen's description of things. But with equal validity, we could describe the relationship between these four aspects and the eternal Logos as sacramental in character. Thus, we could say that Jesus's humanity is the sacrament of the eternal Logos and that the literal meaning of Scripture is the sacrament of the eternal Logos. After all, the Logos has a "real presence" in the incarnate Christ by means of the divine nature and in Scripture through the spiritual meaning of the text. Likewise, we may add, the Logos has a "real presence" in the soul and in the church.

We need to note the implication of this sacramental viewpoint particularly with regard to Holy Scripture. Robert Daly makes the point that there is a "*real* incarnation and hence 'real presence' of the eternal WORD in the scriptures."[50] He goes on to say: "It is thus not mere metaphorical language but precise theological description to speak of the 'sacramentality of the biblical word' according to Origen."[51] It seems to me that Daly is quite right in his observation. We have already seen that the term "mystery" has the sacramental connotation that we have just been tracing in connection with the Word's various incarnations. The events described in the biblical text are mysteries; they are sacraments. That is to say, the eternal Word or Logos of God shows up in them. There is a real presence of this eternal Word in the events that the Bible describes.

That Origen is firmly convinced of this real, sacramental presence of the Word in the Old Testament is something that we can trace throughout the *Commentary on Joshua*. The very fact that Joshua's name in the Septuagint is simply rendered as "Jesus" and that Origen uses this Greek name throughout his homilies enables him to shift back and forth nearly seamlessly from Old Testament type to New Testament reality; from the sacrament of the historical event to the mystical reality of the eternal Word.[52] He starts Homily 1 magnificently with an allusion to Philippians 2:9: "God gave the name that is above every name to our Lord and Savior Jesus Christ. For this 'name that is above every name' is Jesus."[53] Noting that Moses was unable to lead the army and asked Jesus (Joshua) to choose mighty men (Exod. 17:9), Origen comments: "Therefore, when I become acquainted with the name of Jesus for the first time, I also immediately see the symbol of a mystery [*mysterii video sacramentum*]. Indeed, Jesus leads the army."[54] Origen's use of the terms *mysterium* and *sacramentum* right at the outset of his commentary confirms for us the nearly synonymous meaning that these two words carried for the church fathers and the medieval tradition. Throughout his homilies, Origen speaks of the literal sense as the mystery or sacrament of the spiritual sense.[55]

It may be worth our while to go through a few examples, in order to get a sense of how important this sacramental relationship between the divine Word and human words is for Origen. In Homily 11, the Alexandrian preacher comments: "But meanwhile Jesus destroyed the enemies, not teaching cruelty through this, as the heretics think, but representing the *future sacraments* in these affairs, so that when *Jesus destroys those kings* who maintain a reign of sin in us, we can fulfill that which the Apostle said, 'Just as we presented our members to serve iniquity for iniquity, so now let us present our members to serve righteousness for sanctification' [Rom. 6:19]."[56] We may notice in this passage both the paradoxical language of "future sacraments," which we saw Susan Wood borrowing from the Great Tradition, and the seamless way in which Origen moves from the historical to the spiritual meaning when he comments that "Jesus destroys those kings." When he first says that "Jesus destroyed the enemies," Origen's words contain a certain ambiguity: the clause may speak either of Joshua the son of Nun or of Jesus Christ; the Greek identity between the two makes both understandings possible. It is only the rest of the passage that makes clear that Origen is really speaking of Christ. It is Jesus, not Joshua, who destroys our demonic enemies so that we can live holy lives in line with Romans 6.

In Homily 22, Origen observes that Joshua reports three times that the Canaanites live among the people of Ephraim. He then comments that if we investigate these three occurrences carefully, "we shall not doubt that these things were written not so that only a narration of exploits might be transmitted to us [i.e., the historical sense], but so that these things be filled with *divine sacraments* and things worthy of God."[57] The "divine sacraments" speak of the spiritual reality to which the historical accounts point. In the same homily, when Origen notes the command to "purge the Rephaites from among you" (Josh. 17:15), he comments: "We find Rephaites to be interpreted 'slack mothers.' According to that which is said in a mystery [*in sacramento*] concerning the soul as though concerning a woman, there is a certain power in our soul that brings forth perceptions and is, so to speak, the mother of those perceptions."[58] When the power of these perceptions is "slack and languid," this is indicated "under the name 'Rephaites,' so that we may purge ourselves of these languid mothers, who bear weak and useless thoughts."[59] Origen intentionally and explicitly identifies the Rephaites in sacramental fashion.

When in Homily 23 Origen discusses the drawing of lots to divide the conquered cities, he makes the point that this dividing of lots mirrors an angelic drawing of lots in heaven. He then comments: "Insofar as it was permitted, we have dared to offer to you these things concerning the distribution of the lots of the land of Judah by the invitation of Scripture, which calls Jerusalem and Mount Zion heavenly, and the rest of those places that are written to be in heaven. This gave us the opportunity to remark about all these passages because heavenly mysteries are described in them."[60] The reference to "heavenly mysteries" in connection with the various place names implies, according to Origen, that one should not think that the book of Joshua relates something "worthless" when it presents us with these many proper names. "Rather, know that ineffable things are contained in these mysteries and things greater than either the human word is able to utter or the mortal sense of hearing to hear."[61] Earthly events such as the drawing of lots, as well as the names of cities mentioned in Joshua thus turn out to be sacramental "mysteries" of heavenly realities.

As he discusses the detailed description of the inheritance that the various sons of Levi receive, he interrupts himself in Homily 25 with the words:

> Who is able to follow and to comprehend all these things? Who can even remember and pay attention to the order of the mysteries [*mysteriorum*]? But if, according to the letter alone, we can explain the difficult text of the narration and unfold the confusion either of places or of persons that are bound together in the story, what do we say concerning those sacraments [*sacramentis*] that are depicted through this, and in which the distributions of a future inheritance are dimly sketched?[62]

Again, Origen uses the terms "mysteries" and "sacraments" to denote the heavenly, eternal realities given in earthly, this-worldly descriptions.

Finally, in the next homily, when he discusses the trans-Jordanian tribes building an altar in imitation of that of Judah (Josh. 22:10–20), Origen first recounts the historical event, and then immediately adds: "But let us see *what sacrament* lies within this deed."[63] He then proceeds with the spiritual interpretation of this particular chapter. The "sacrament" is obviously the spiritual explanation of the passage.

These examples from Origen's homilies on Joshua present us with a rather impressive number of occurrences of the words "sacrament" and "mystery." There is little doubt that for Origen the words of the biblical text, while they relate historical events, also carry a deeper meaning, one that is located in heaven and refers to Jesus Christ, the eternal Son of God, himself. It is important to note that this sacramental interpretation is thoroughly christological. We need to keep this in mind in connection with the objections that we noted at the beginning of the essay regarding Origen's allegorizing. Origen, I indicated, is often viewed as a moralist, who jumps straight from the Old Testament to how we should live. Certainly, Origen is concerned with the virtuous habits of the Christian life. But he is also thoroughly christological in his exegesis. The sacramental meaning of the historical event refers first and foremost to Jesus, who himself is the Incarnation of the eternal Logos. Origen is a "man of the church," a *vir ecclesiasticus*. And as such, his prime concern is Jesus Christ. The Alexandrian tradition stemming from Origen is thus a sacramental tradition that has Christology for its starting-point.

History's Rightful Place

At this point, we need to ask the question, does history receive its rightful place in Origen's sacramental reading of Joshua? In addressing this question, it is probably wise to think carefully about what we mean by history's "rightful place." If we regard as the purpose of biblical exegesis to find out what the human author really meant, this often tends to imply, as the nineteenth-century Oxford critic Benjamin Jowett famously put it in 1860, that we read Scripture "like any other book."[64] Seeing that authorial intent is a historical matter, the resolution to such a quest inevitably yields varying degrees of probability. If, with such an understanding of biblical interpretation, we ask whether Origen gave history its "rightful place," the answer must be negative. Origen is singularly *un*concerned with the kinds of historical questions modern scholars tend to put to the text. He is almost oblivious to what the original author may have meant with the text of the book of Joshua. The reason is this: Origen doesn't so much look backward as forward. For Origen, biblical interpretation is not first and foremost a historical discipline. Such an approach would have struck him as an oddly reductionistic enterprise.

Furthermore, when it comes to history itself, unlike many modern historians, Origen does not reduce history to measurable cause-and-effect, to that which we can observe with the senses. This means that he regards history as open to a providential ordering of events. His sermons are predicated on the notion that the history of salvation is divine in character. He does not begin with attempting to ascertain the historicity of particular events. Instead, he takes them for granted (most of the time), and he reads them as guided by God himself.

When, for example, Origen turns in Homily 23 to the drawing of the lots for the seven tribes as described in Joshua 17–19, he engages in a theological discussion of providence. He begins by discussing the drawing of lots in Leviticus 16, where one lot was taken for God and another for the scapegoat (Lev. 16:8).[65] Origen observes that Caleb was assigned a share *not* by lot, but "according to the commandment of the Lord" (Josh. 14:13).[66] Many others on the west side of the Jordan River, however, get their portions assigned through the casting of lots. And Origen adds the theologically weighty comment that "that lot is not tossed by chance, but according to that which was predestined by God."[67] Origen then goes through several additional biblical occurrences of the lot: Jonah was selected by lot to be cast into the sea; Solomon appeals to the lot in the book of Proverbs; and the apostles filled the place of Judas by casting the lot. Again, Origen concludes that "when prayer preceded, it was no longer by chance but by providence that the lot announced divine judgment."[68] Next, he

CRUX: Fall 2012/Vol. 48, No. 3

relates this providential ordering of the lot to Christology: "But still I sought in the New Testament if anywhere the lot is mentioned in relation to Christ or to the Church, or even to mystic things that seem to relate to the soul."[69] He then observes that several New Testament passages speak of the believers' predestination "by lot."[70] Origen insists that these passages, too, should be understood not just in their historical sense: "But according to the inner understanding, as Paul seems to indicate when he says, 'in the portion of the lot of the saints' [Col. 1:12], and 'called by lot in Christ' [Eph. 1:11], it must be seen whether perchance the lot is drawn not only among humans, but also among the celestial powers."[71] All of Scripture, including the New Testament, is subject to spiritual interpretation for Origen. The New Testament, too, points to eternal realities.

When we draw lots here on earth, the results are in line with lots drawn in heaven. This explains, according to Origen, why Deuteronomy 32:8–9 can say that God divided the nations and fixed the boundaries of the nations "according to the number of the angels of God." "We must not think," insists Origen, "that it was by accident that it indeed fell to one angel to receive by lot one nation, for example, that of the Egyptians, but to another, the nation of the Idumeans, and to another, the nation of the Moabites, and to another, India or every single nation on earth."[72] Origen thus arrives at the conclusion "that not even for a single one of us does anything come to pass except by a lot of this kind that is dispensed by the judgment of God."[73] It now becomes clear that when by lot Benjamin receives Jerusalem and Mount Zion, this is not just an accidental matter: "Doubtless, it is because the nature of that heavenly Jerusalem established it that the earthly Jerusalem, which preserved a figure and form of the heavenly one, ought to be given to none other than Benjamin."[74] (Origen here has in mind Hebrews 10:1 and 12:22, which he has just quoted.) It is divine providence that arranges human affairs by heavenly lots, so that earthly arrangements are in line with heavenly ones.

It should be clear at this point that history is not insignificant for Origen. We may even say that he has a more exalted view of history than do many modern historical exegetes. The reason is precisely that he refuses to reduce history to immanent cause-and-effect. Because history is for Origen a matter of providential ordering, it is much more than just inner-worldly cause-and-effect observable by the senses. A view of history as purely autonomous and this-worldly would have struck him as terribly reductionistic. History, to Origen, has significance because it is the outcome of God's eternal providential ordering.

It seems unlikely, therefore, that when Origen allegorizes, he means to suggest thereby that the historical event never occurred. His spiritual reading can hardly be meant to *deny* history, at least not across the board. Both Origen's sacramental understanding of interpretation and his insistence on the providential ordering of history militate against this. If it is *historical events* that carry a sacramental dimension, then this means that the spiritual reality is present *in historical events*. And if God orders history providentially, then, again, this implies an acknowledgement of its significance. Accordingly, Henri de Lubac, in his book on Origen's biblical interpretation, shows at length that usually Origen affirms the historicity of the events. "All that happened," explains de Lubac, "happened 'in mystery': but the mystery presupposes the real event. One must believe 'the testimony of the history.'"[75]

In his book *On First Principles*, Origen distinguishes a threefold interpretation, and he makes clear that *each* of the three levels is integral to a full-orbed understanding of the text:

> One must therefore pourtray the meaning of the sacred writings in a threefold way upon one's own soul, so that the simple man may be edified by what we may call

the flesh of the scripture, this name being given to the obvious interpretation; while the man who has made some progress may be edified by its soul, as it were; and the man who is perfect and like those mentioned by the apostle; "We speak wisdom among the perfect; yet a wisdom not of this world, nor of the rulers of this world, which are coming to nought; but we speak of God's wisdom that hath been hidden, which God foreordained before the worlds unto our glory" [1 Cor. 2:6–7]—this man may be edified by the spiritual law [cf. Rom. 7:14], which has "a shadow of the good things to come" [Heb. 10:1]. For just as man consists of body, soul and spirit, so in the same way does the scripture, which has been prepared by God to be given for man's salvation.[76]

There are three levels of meaning, according to Origen: the literal, the moral, and the spiritual. These three levels correspond to the various aspects of the human person: the literal level corresponds to the body; the moral level to the soul; and the spiritual level to the spirit.[77] The historical level of interpretation is part and parcel of the overall pattern with its various levels. For Origen, one cannot interpret Scripture without doing justice to history. The common assumption, therefore, that allegory is a jumping *away from* history is, to put it bluntly, simply based on a lack of knowledge of the fathers. Once we start reading the fathers for ourselves, we come to recognize that historical realities are an integral part—although by no means the most important part—of the reading of the text.

This is not to say that Origen never devalued or even discounted the literal meaning. There "are certain passages of scripture which, as we shall show in what follows, have no bodily sense at all," he insists in *On First Principles*.[78] Sometimes,

"the scripture wove into the story something which did not happen, occasionally something which could not happen, and occasionally something which might have happened but in fact did not."[79] Even when speaking of the Gospels and the writings of the apostles, Origen comments that "the history even of these is not everywhere pure, events being woven together in the bodily sense without having actually happened; nor do the law and the commandments contained therein entirely declare what is reasonable."[80] On Origen's understanding, the Spirit sometimes included along with the historical account descriptions of things that were either contradictory or immoral, and which God thus intended as obstacles, deliberately placed in the text in order to drive people to the benefit of a spiritual reading.

We see such non-historical readings also in the *Homilies on Joshua*. A few examples will suffice to clarify the point. In Homily 7, Origen comments: "I would like to inquire of the Jews and of those who are called Christians, but who still preserve the Jewish interpretation of Scriptures, how they explain that 'Rahab the prostitute was joined to the house of Israel up to this very day' [Josh. 6:25]. How is Rahab said to be 'joined up to this very day'?"[81] Similarly, when Joshua defeats the alliance of Jabin, King of Hazor, he destroys all his people— "so that no one remained there who might recover" (Josh. 11:11)—and he hamstrings their horses. Noticing the order of events, *first* the destruction of every single person and *then* the hamstringing of their horses, Origen comments in Homily 15:

> Concerning this, we say first of all to those who wish these things to be understood only according to the letter, that if any of the enemies had survived, it seemed reasonable that the horses be hamstrung so that no one could use them for flight. But here, when it is said that no one was left among the enemies who could

take a breath, why were the horses still commanded to be hamstrung, especially those that were able to be of use and service to the victors?[82]

Origen takes the logical improbability of these passages as sufficient reason to move to a spiritual reading. He does the same thing on at least five other occasions.[83] The reason is, no doubt, that his relative neglect of history (or, we might say, his urge to get beyond history to the spiritual meaning) is such that he cannot bother taking the time to investigate possible solutions to the apparent contradictions that he finds in the literal meaning of the text. I don't think there is an adequate defense for such neglect. But if we ask which neglect is more serious, the nearly wholesale neglect of spiritual levels of interpretation in a great deal of modern historical exegesis or the occasional neglect of history in Origen and other practitioners of allegorical exegesis, the answer seems to me fairly evident.

From History to Spirit: Biblical Rationale
This leads us to the question: on what biblical basis does Origen move from history to spirit? What is his rationale for this sacramental approach to Scripture? Doesn't such a move from history to spirit lead to a supersessionism in which the New Testament simply supersedes and replaces the Old? Put sharply, what real use can Origen possibly have for the Old Testament? Of course, we have already seen his main motive for the move from history to spirit: he holds to a sacramental view of history and of the Scriptures. Furthermore, we have seen that on occasion, when the text appears problematic, Origen jumps straight to the spiritual meaning without worrying about the historical event. So, we know why it is that Origen saw multiple levels of meaning in the text: his sacramental view of reality demanded as much. But the question we have not yet asked is this: how does Origen ground this sacramental view biblically? Does the Bible support his allegorical exegesis?

Interestingly, Origen's homilies often discuss and justify his hermeneutical moves as he presents his understanding of the text. On various occasions, the text's very meaning, according to Origin, refers to the principle of allegorizing. In other words, he sees the biblical text as addressing the question of interpretation. Such is the case in Homily 2, when God promises Joshua (or Jesus) that he will give him every place, "wherever [he] will ascend with the soles of [his] feet" (Josh. 1:3).[84] Origen insists:

> The letter of the law is placed on the ground and lies down below. On no occasion, then, does the one who follows the letter of the Law ascend. But if you are able to rise from the letter to the spirit and also ascend from history to a higher understanding, then truly you have ascended the lofty and high place that you will receive from God as your inheritance.[85]

The very phrase "ascend with the soles of your feet" carries, for Origen, a hermeneutical principle, namely, that we are to ascend from the historical to the spiritual level. Apparently, when we read the text allegorically, the allegorical level gives us the justification for this practice of allegorical exegesis in which we have just engaged.[86]

It may seem hard to avoid the conclusion that this involves a form of circular reasoning: Origen assumes the results of spiritual interpretation to justify its practice; it is an allegorical reading of Joshua's ascent "with the soles of [his] feet" that shores up his allegorical approach. I am not so sure, however, that Origen asks us to take his reading of Joshua 1:3 in a strictly logical or demonstrative sense. I suspect that his desire to delight the reader and to bring to the fore readings that allude to God's eternal beauty drives him (as well as other fathers) to engage in this sort of exegetical practice.[87] Exegetes such as Origen would hardly consider this particular reading of Joshua 1:3 as the definitive meaning of the text. Instead,

Origen would likely regard it as one of many possible readings, a reading that particularly delighted him, that was consonant with the overall faith of the church, and that made sense only if one was already convinced of the need for spiritual interpretation.

Origen often goes beyond such self-referential Old Testament interpretations to New Testament texts that, to his mind, directly assert the requirement of spiritual interpretation. I do not need to rehearse these New Testament passages in detail.[88] When Origen turns to passages such as 1 Corinthians 10:4 ("For they drank from the supernatural Rock which followed them, and the Rock was Christ," RSV), Galatians 4:24 ("Now this is an allegory [ἀλληγούμεν]: these women are two covenants," RSV), and others, he simply steps into the exegetical precedent set by the apostle Paul himself. As Peter Martens puts it: "Throughout his entire career, Origen repeatedly invoked Paul's name as the practitioner and guide par excellence to the allegorical interpretation of Israel's Scriptures."[89] In doing so, Origen wasn't particularly unique. Other church fathers often used the same passages. The reason is that, like them, Origen is preoccupied with the spiritual progress that his hearers must make, a spiritual progress that he sees expressed in various New Testament passages. But again, this spiritual progress does not come at the expense of the letter. In some sense it is true that the letter and the law are disregarded: Moses "cannot lead the army" into the Promised Land.[90] Jesus needs to do this. And "if we do not understand how Moses dies, we shall not be able to understand how Jesus reigns."[91] Origen goes on at some length about the rites of the law having become obsolete now that Jesus holds the leadership. But he immediately adds that the law does hold its place among Christians. Appealing to *The Assumption of Moses*, Origen comments that

> two Moses were seen: one alive in the spirit, another dead in the body. Doubtless, in this was foreshadowed that, if you consider the letter of the Law empty and void of all those things we have mentioned above [the Old Testament sacrificial rites and the like], you have the Moses who is dead in the body; but if you are able to draw back the veil from the Law [2 Cor. 3:16] and perceive that "the Law is spiritual" [Rom. 7:14], you have the Moses who lives in the spirit.[92]

For Origen, Moses is both dead and alive. As long as we read him spiritually, he remains alive for us. So, yes, in an important sense, the New Testament does supersede the Old, just as the new covenant supersedes the old. At the same time, however, the New Testament also renders the fullest and truest meaning of the Old Testament, by drawing out its deepest mystery, its sacramental meaning. And in so doing, Origen spots a greater treasure in the Old Testament than it had been possible to find prior to the coming of Christ.[93]

It is not the purpose of this essay either to defend each and every exegetical choice that Origen makes, or to suggest that he investigates the historical meaning of the Scriptures with the kind of care with which one perhaps would have liked him to. Still, the common objections to Origen's interpretation of Scripture remain largely unconvincing because they are predicated on a view of history that approaches it without regard either for the providential ordering of history or for its sacramental functioning. It is because he recognizes this sacramental function of history—as well as of the Scriptures recording historical events—that Origen sees in history much greater significance than do his modern-day detractors.[94] ✗

Notes

1. Origen, *On First Principles*, trans. and ed. G.W. Butterworth and Henri de Lubac (1936; repr., Gloucester, MA: Smith, 1973), 4.2.4 (pp. 275–77).

2. R.P.C. Hanson, *Allegory and Event: A Study of the Sources and Significance of Origen's Interpretation of Scripture* (1959; repr., Louisville: Westminster John

Knox, 2002).

3. Henri de Lubac, *History and Spirit: The Understanding of Scripture according to Origen*, trans. Anne Englund Nash with Juvenal Merriell (San Francisco: Ignatius, 2007). For a more recent positive evaluation of Origen, see Peter W. Martens, *Origen and Scripture: The Contours of the Exegetical Life* (Oxford: Oxford University Press, 2012).

4. Cf. Hans Boersma, *Heavenly Participation: The Weaving of a Sacramental Tapestry* (Grand Rapids, MI: Eerdmans, 2011), 137–53.

5. This point is made particularly eloquently by Peter W. Martens, "Origen against History? Reconsidering the Critique of Allegory," *Modern Theology* 28 (2012): 635–56.

6. Origen, *Homilies on Joshua*, trans. Barbara J. Bruce, ed. Cynthia White, The Fathers of the Church 105 (Washington, DC: Catholic University of America Press, 2002), 5.5 (p. 63). Cf. also ibid., 7.5 (p. 79).

7. Ibid. Cf. Josh. 5:2; 1 Cor. 10:4.

8. Origen, *Homilies on Joshua* 9.4 (p. 99).

9. Ibid., 13.1 (p. 125).

10. Ibid., 15.6 (p. 149).

11. This is largely the approach that Jason Byassee takes in regard to St. Augustine in his otherwise fine study, *Praise Seeking Understanding: Reading the Psalms with Augustine* (Grand Rapids, MI: Eerdmans, 2009).

12. Origen, *Homilies of Joshua* 17.1 (p. 157).

13. Ibid. Cf. 2.1 (pp. 37–38).

14. Ibid., 17.1 (p. 157).

15. Ibid. (p. 158).

16. Cf. Philip J. Lee, *Against the Protestant Gnostics* (New York: Oxford University Press, 1987), 11. For Origen's relationship to Gnostic groups, see David Brakke, *The Gnostics: Myth, Ritual, and Diversity in Early Christianity* (Cambridge, MA: Harvard University Press, 2012), 128–32.

17. Walter Wink, *Cracking the Gnostic Code: The Powers in Gnosticism*, Society of Biblical Literature Monograph Series 46 (Atlanta, GA: Scholars, 1993), 16.

18. De Lubac, *History and Spirit*, 56.

19. Ibid., 54. See also Origen, *Homilies* 7.7 (p. 83); 12.3 (p. 123).

20. De Lubac, *History and Spirit*, 57.

21. Origen, *Homilies* 10.2 (p. 111). The Septuagint renders Joshua's name as "Jesus," which is the Greek name that Origen uses here and elsewhere.

22. Ibid., 10.3 (p. 112).

23. Cf. Origen, *On First Principles* 4.2.1 (pp. 269–71). Here Origen takes issue first with "the hard-hearted and ignorant members of the circumcision," then with "the members of the heretical sects," and finally with "the simpler of those who claim to belong to the Church" for their literalist reading of the Old Testament Scriptures.

24. I do not mean to suggest that violence can never be justified. I have argued elsewhere that I think it does, in fact, play a role in the divine economy (*Violence, Hospitality, and the Cross: Reappropriating the Atonement Tradition* [Grand Rapids, MI: Baker Academic, 2004]). Still, if we restrict ourselves to a literal reading of Joshua, we miss out on typological/ allegorical elements in the text that prevent us from taking elements such as incitements to genocide as timeless principles valid for all times.

25. Susan K. Wood, *Spiritual Exegesis and the Church in the Theology of Henri de Lubac* (Grand Rapids, MI: Eerdmans, 1998), 39.

26. Ibid.

27. I discuss this in more detail in *Heavenly Participation*, 21–23.

28. Robert J. Daly, foreword to Origen, *Spirit and Fire: A Thematic Anthology of His Writings*, ed. Hans Urs von Balthasar, trans. Robert J. Daly (1984; repr., Washington, DC: Catholic University Press, 2001), xiv; emphasis original.

29. It seems to me that the "incarnations" in Scripture and in the soul can only be termed "incarnations" in an analogical sense.

30. Daly, foreword to *Spirit and Fire*, xiv.

31. De Lubac, *History and Spirit*, 397. The quotation is from Origen, *Commentary on the Song of Songs* 2.

32. De Lubac, *History and Spirit*, 398.

33. Ibid.

34. A full response to the objection of arbitrariness lies beyond the scope of this essay but would have to include discussion of the following elements: (1) the wide variety of results yielded by historical exegesis, which opens it up no less than the church fathers to the charge of arbitrariness; (2) the often remarkable similarities in approach and actual exegetical outcome among a broad range of premodern interpreters; (3) the church's liturgy and "rule of faith" as setting boundaries for what constitutes proper interpretation; (4) the Spirit's guidance of the faithful in the church in adhering faithfully to the divine intentions of the church's book; (5) the function of "profitability" as simply being more important to the believer than arriving at the exact authorial intent; and (6) many premodern interpreters' openness to multiple interpretations of one particular text.

35. Origen, *Spirit and Fire*, 389 (p. 155).

36. Cf. de Lubac, *History and Spirit*, 68–73.

37. See especially Henri de Lubac, *Catholicism: Christ and the Common Destiny of Man*, trans. Lancelot C. Sheppard and Elizabeth Englund (San Francisco: Ignatius, 1988).

38. De Lubac makes the point that also the entire universe is the "subject of spiritual interpretation" (*History and Spirit*, 401), so that it, too, is an incarnation of the Logos (ibid., 401–6). Furthermore, since the Eucharist is also the body of Christ, the bread and wine of the Eucharist are types or symbols of the church (ibid., 406–15). Thus, the Eucharist, too, is an incarnation of the Word.

39. Balthasar, in Origen, *Fire and Spirit*, 148.

40. Origen, *Fire and Spirit*, 368–75 (pp. 148–52).

41. St. Augustine's *totus Christus* theology— with Christ and the church together forming the "whole Christ"—functions in a similar manner. Cf. Hans Boersma, "The Church Fathers' Spiritual Interpretation of the Psalms," in *Living Waters from*

Ancient Springs: Essays in Honor of Cornelis Van Dam, ed. Jason Van Vliet (Eugene, OR.: Pickwick / Wipf & Stock, 2011), 41–55.

42. Origen, *Fire and Spirit*, 407 (p. 170).

43. De Lubac, *History and Spirit*, 412. De Lubac's comment can be interpreted in a way that would render it acceptable. Still, it gives a one-sided impression, as his comment ignores the distinction between Christ and his church, along with his lordship over the church.

44. Ibid.

45. Ibid.

46. Ibid., 105. Cf. ibid., 385–96; Hans Boersma, *Nouvelle Théologie and Sacramental Ontology: A Return to Mystery* (Oxford: Oxford University Press, 2009), 161.

47. De Lubac, *History and Spirit*, 385.

48. Ibid.

49. Origen, *Comm. on John* 10.35; quoted in de Lubac, *History and Spirit*, 412.

50. Daly, foreword to *Spirit and Fire*, xiv–xv.

51. Ibid. Frances M. Young makes a similar point when she insists: "The biblical narratives, read imaginatively rather than literally, but accorded an authority greater than the merely metaphorical, can become luminous of a divine reality beyond human expression. This is not so much allegorical as sacramental" (*Biblical Exegesis and the Formation of Christian Culture* [1997; repr., Peabody, MA: Hendrickson, 2002], 143–44). While I am not persuaded by the differentiation between "allegorical" and "sacramental," Young's overall argument for a sacramental understanding of language (throughout her chapter on "The Sacrament of Language"; ibid., 140–60) is certainly insightful.

52. The Greek identity between Joshua and Jesus is employed both by Justin Martyr and by Origen. See John J. O'Keefe and R.R. Reno, *Sanctified Vision: An Introduction to Early Christian Interpretation of the Bible* (Baltimore: Johns Hopkins University Press, 2005), 74–78.

53. Origen, *Homilies on Joshua* 1.1 (p. 26).

54. Ibid., 1.1 (p. 27).

55. Cf. also Origen, *Spirit and Fire*, 161–69 (pp. 89–90).

56. Origen, *Homilies on Joshua* 11.6 (p. 119); emphasis added.

57. Ibid., 22.1 (p. 189); emphasis added.

58. Ibid., 22.4 (p. 192). The name "Rephaites" appears to be derived from the verb רפה, meaning to sink, drop, relax, or slacken.

59. Ibid.

60. Ibid., 23.4 (p. 201).

61. Ibid. (p. 202).

62. Ibid., 25.4 (pp. 212–13).

63. Ibid., 26.3 (p. 218); emphasis added.

64. Cf. James Barr, "Jowett and the 'Original Meaning' of Scripture," *Religious Studies* 18 (1982): 433–37.

65. Origen, *Homilies on Joshua* 23.1 (p. 195).

66. Ibid., 23.1 (p. 196).

67. Ibid.

68. Ibid., 23.2 (p. 197).

69. Ibid.

70. Ibid. Eph. 1:11–12; Col. 1:12. Eph. 1:11 uses the verb κληρόω ("to cast a lot"); Col. 1:12 speaks of a "share in the allotment" (κλῆρος).

71. Ibid., 23.3 (p. 198).

72. Ibid. (pp. 198–99).

73. Ibid. (p. 199).

74. Ibid., 23.4 (p. 200).

75. De Lubac, *History and Spirit*, 106. I am inclined to think that de Lubac overstates his case somewhat. As we will see, there are instances where Origen does deny the historicity of the events narrated in Joshua.

76. Origen, *On First Principles* 4.2.4 (pp. 275–76).

77. We may well wish to criticize both the order of the three levels of interpretation and Origen's linking of these levels to the human constitution. After all, by placing the moral level before the spiritual level, Origen gives at least the impression that we may arrive at the moral meaning without being concerned with Christology. At the same time, we need to keep in mind that in his actual exegesis, Origen often doesn't move from the historical via the moral to the spiritual. Instead, as de Lubac has made clear, most often Origen moves straight from the historical to the spiritual. See de Lubac's discussion in *History and Spirit*, 159–71. Cf. Boersma, *Nouvelle Théologie*, 164–68.

78. Origen, *On First Principles* 4.2.5 (p. 277).

79. Ibid., 4.2.9 (p. 286).

80. Ibid. (p. 287).

81. Origen, *Homilies on Joshua* 7.5 (p. 79).

82. Ibid., 15.2 (p. 139).

83. Ibid., 6.1 (p. 70); 15.7 (p. 150); 16.1 (p. 152); 20.4 (p. 179); 21.1 (p. 184).

84. Ibid., 2.3 (p. 39).

85. Ibid.

86. Cf. also the interpretation of Josh. 5:2 in ibid., 5.5 (p. 63); and of Josh. 15:17–19 in ibid., 20.6 (p. 182).

87. Cf. Byassee, *Praise Seeking Understanding*, 97–148.

88. In his homilies on Joshua, Origen refers to John 5:46 (18.2 [p. 164]); Rom. 7:14 (which he mentions no less than five times); 1 Cor. 10:4 (5.4 [pp. 63–64]; 15.3 [p. 144]); 1 Cor. 10:11 (mentioned four times); 2 Cor. 3:5 (also used several times); 2 Cor. 3:14–15 (3.1 [p. 41]); Gal. 4:22–24 (9.8 [p. 103]); Heb. 8:5 (17.1 [p. 157]; 17.2 [p. 160]); Heb. 12:22 (23.4 [pp. 200–201]).

89. Martens, *Origen*, 158.

90. Origen, *Homilies on Joshua* 1.1 (p. 27).

91. Ibid., 2.1 (p. 37). Origen here comments on Josh. 1:2.

92. Ibid., 2.1 (p. 38).

93. For a more elaborate exposition of Origen's understanding of the relationship between Old and New Testaments, see de Lubac, *History and Spirit*, 190–204.

94. I want to express my appreciation to Peter W. Martens for his insightful comments on an earlier draft of this essay.

Father and Son: John Calvin and Communion

Julie Canlis

If there is any "methodology" that I learned from Jim Houston, as a student of his from 1996–2000, it was to fight reductionism in any form ... particularly as one reads the great Christian authors of the past. "We are all standing on the shoulders of giants," he would remind us again and again, as he refused to take cheap shots at Augustine's trinitarianism, or even at suspects such as Meister Eckhart. ("The heretics are always protesting some reductionism—we must pay attention to them!") But what I did not fully realize was that this methodological generosity was, in fact, the way in which Jim related to all humans, living or dead. Jim did not treat anyone en masse ... not even dead theologians! To our amazement (and sometimes confusion), he would spend a three-hour lecture delving into the history, foibles, cultural background, and childhood of these Christian "giants," modeling for us a non-reductive approach to reading and to life.

The golden thread guiding it all was Jim's quest for the *personal*—whether in his relationship to past authors or current students. He reads personally, he lives personally, he teaches personally. In class, he always pointed out that it is the authors who are most "human" in their writings who are also the most perennial. So Jim had us reading all over the continents and centuries, on a wild goose chase for that elusive element of the "human" and the "personal." (Reminder: the wild goose is an ancient Celtic symbol for the Holy Spirit!) Through it all, Jim continually challenged us to use our minds to the utmost, while training us to be truly personal and truly human ourselves—which is nothing less than being a self for the other.

This address was delivered earlier this year in Dublin, at the 50th International Eucharistic Congress of the Catholic Church, which also was celebrating the fiftieth anniversary of Vatican II. It bears the marks of many fruitful years of discussion with Jim, and in many ways is a tribute to his influence in my life.

&

Charles Taylor, in his wonderful tome *A Secular Age*, writes,

> None of us could ever grasp alone everything that is involved in our alienation from God and his action to bring us back. But there are a great many of us, scattered through history, who have had some powerful sense of some facet of this drama. Together we can live it more fully than any one of us could alone.[1]

Today you have invited John Calvin—the very same John Calvin who allegedly walked the halls of the Collège de Montaigu alongside Ignatius of Loyola—to speak to you of his unique sense of some "facet of the drama." Even more bravely, you have asked John Calvin to speak to you on the subject of communion, as one who himself broke communion with the Catholic Church five hundred years ago. You are, in fact,

Julie Canlis won the Templeton Award for Theological Promise in 2007 for her work on John Calvin, published recently as Calvin's Ladder, *which won a 2011* Christianity Today *Award of Merit. She is a part-time lecturer and teaches sunday school at a small Church of Scotland parish where her husband, Matt, is minister. Together, they are raising four young children in rural Scotland.*

following Charles Taylor's further advice to not "reach for the weapons of polemic" but instead to "listen for a voice which we could never have assumed ourselves, whose tone might have been forever unknown to us if we hadn't strained to understand it."[2] Thank you for straining to understand. It is an honour to be here.

Many recent documents and theological treatises about communion begin with communion as a fundamental human longing, which (theologically) I believe is true. Calvin would agree wholeheartedly with this. He writes, "And, indeed, there is nothing in which man excels the lower animals unless it be his spiritual communion with God in the hope of a blessed eternity."[3] But after rewriting and rearranging for decades, Calvin did not begin his final edition of the *Institutes of the Christian Religion* with communion as an anthropological fact or as a fundamental human longing, even as his work radiates its reality. Rather, the 1559 *Institutes* follows the order of the Apostle's Creed, which reflects the triune activity to bring humanity into God's own communion.

In place of the original catechetical structure of the *Institutes*, a creedal, trinitarian one emerged comprised of four books: Father, Son, Spirit, and Church. As a result of this change, we begin to see a subtle shift in Calvin's approach to theology—perhaps even a shift in his spirituality. Calvin restructured the *Institutes* such that God's triune communion sets the stage. It is not Scripture, or God's unity, or the chronology of predestination that is dealt with first (although later redactors of Calvin would unfortunately restructure this), but for Calvin, it is the story of God triunely relating *to us* that frames his theological vision. It is God, not the human being, who sets the communion stage. We enter into a drama already well under way. So from the very beginning, before the first page is turned, Calvin's challenge is for us to wake up to the personalness (the communion) of God all around us. And it is in this personal, relational manner that we are led in to the *Institutes*.

Now Barth was a huge admirer of Calvin. He was exposed to him on a sustained level in the early 1920s, when he was assigned to teach a series of lectures on what was then an unknown subject to him: the Reformed confessions. During this formative time, he wrote to Eduard Thurneyson:

> Calvin is a cataract, a primeval forest, a demonic power, something directly down from the Himalaya, absolutely Chinese, strange, mythological; I lack completely the means, the suction cups, even to assimilate this phenomenon, not to speak of presenting it adequately. What I receive is only a thin little stream and what I can then give out again is only a yet thinner extract of this little stream. I could gladly and profitably set myself down and spend all the rest of my life just with Calvin.[4]

Barth took Calvin's emphasis (as typified in his final restructuring of the *Institutes*) and turned it into a hermeneutical principle to do theology "from above" rather than "from below." Despite Barth's earlier theology, in which human questions about God (and indeed, even the human *in*capacity to speak of God) framed the discussion, the later Barth deemed this to border on a natural theology. One could not, *must not*, begin from the existential situation of humanity—even if it is a declaration of humanity's finitude and need for God. Only God can be a proper point of departure for theology; it is God, not we humans and our situation, that must set the terms for doing theology. Thus saith Barth.

Barth reflects the Protestant "reticence" to start with nature and ascend (or move from that starting point) unto God, but Calvin is not averse to doing so—as long as it is not turned into an anthropological principle. Speaking generally, the Protestant fear is that if one begins with common human experience, depending on one's

42

century and culture, it is all too easy to pour one's qualifications and preconceived notions into this and project it onto God. For example, it has been said that the history of theological interpretation of the *imago Dei* is better seen as a cultural history than as a theological one. We can't help it: we are in-carnate, enfleshed people shaped by our relationships, context, and the glorious gift of life in a particular place, in a particular time on earth. So perhaps it is not too surprising that the *imago Dei* was perceived as rational capacity in the fourth century (Augustine), free choice in the twelfth (Bernard), vitiated and near-absent in the sixteenth (Reformers), and today, I have seen it construed as our capacity to be ecological caretakers. As a result of this, for better and for worse, the Protestant instinct is to be reticent about nature, experience, and all things "human" (even the longing for communion) without first taking one's bearings from God and his revelation in Christ. But the question remains, can this really be done at all? Can we pretend to be people of the Word and not also of the world we inhabit? Can this not easily lead into a Gnosticism of its own? This is, perhaps, the Protestant (particularly post-Kantian) predicament.

Calvin is not so oppositional, a fact over which Barth himself marveled:

> As remarkable as it may sound when I say this about Calvin, he thinks initially not from God but from the human person and his situation. Yet the situation of humanity cannot be considered with any seriousness at all without thinking immediately of God. For what purpose is the human created?[5]

This flexibility of Calvin, to think equally from the situation of the human and from the situation of the divine, is the fruit of two factors in his life: his pre-modern context[6] and his robust theology of the Holy Spirit. (Although it is obvious that Barth did not share the former with Calvin, it is highly probable that he did not share the latter either!) To begin with the Trinity is not a denial of human experience but is *precisely Calvin's way to approach human experience.* Even his opening sentences of the *Institutes* reflect his desire to do justice to both human experience and divine revelation concurrently. Calvin says,

> Our wisdom, in so far as it ought to be deemed true and solid Wisdom, consists almost entirely of two parts: the knowledge of God and of ourselves. But as these are connected together by many ties, *it is not easy to determine which of the two precedes and gives birth to the other.* For, in the first place, no man can survey himself without forthwith turning his thoughts towards the God in whom he lives and moves; because it is perfectly obvious, that the endowments which we possess cannot possibly be from ourselves; nay, that our very being is nothing else than subsistence in God alone. In the second place, those blessings which unceasingly distil to us from heaven, are like streams conducting us to the fountain. Here, again, the infinitude of good which resides in God becomes more apparent from our poverty.[7]

When it comes to defining communion with God, Calvin knows himself to be working with shadows and figures. Calvin's opinion is that we cannot truly know what communion is by looking at the Bible's description of the first humans. Calvin remarks, "That original excellence and nobility which we have recounted would be of no profit to us … until God … appeared as Redeemer in the person of the only begotten Son."[8] Neither can we peer behind the veil and discern the communion of the Godhead itself. Calvin warns that those who "indulge their curiosity … enter into a labyrinth."[9] So if we cannot look at humans to understand communion aright, nor penetrate the ineffable mystery of the Godhead to understand communion, to whom shall we go?

Although the trinitarian communion will always be a mystery, Calvin is emphatic that there are aspects of it that have been flung open to us in Christ. He says, "Christ alone is the mirror in which we can contemplate that which [we cannot clearly see for] ourselves."[10] And this is where I get to the heart of Calvin's contribution to the ecumenical discussion of communion: communion must take as its starting point Christ's earthly relation with his Father. This is the ontological entry-point to our experience of communion— whether it be our communion with God, with one another, or within the structures of the ecclesia. Calvin understands this primary relationship— that of Father and Son—to be at the root of all reality. It took me multiple reads of the *Institutes* and commentaries to realize what Calvin is doing: he is painting the whole biblical story in terms of a *father and son*. We humans fit into this prior dynamic. T. F. Torrance, that famed Scottish theologian who was a student of Calvin, notes much the same thing when he says that "God was not always eternally Creator but he was always and eternally *Father*."[11] The human story does not unfold within God generally, but the story of humanity unfolds within a particular, concrete aspect of God's communion, of Father and Son.

The Old Testament: The Fatherhood of God

Indulge me for a moment, by allowing me to paint in broad brushstrokes just how pervasive this Father-Son communion is for Calvin, colouring everything he has to say about the human story. In Calvin's *Institutes*, Adam is called a "son" who is surrounded with signs of the "paternal goodness"[12] of God. Adam's glory lies not in his superhuman perfections but rather that he is a "partaker" of God for everything he enjoys in the garden. Human perfection, in other words, lies in communion with God. To be human, Adam needs God. This is Adam's glory—the way he was designed— not a deficiency due to sin.

So what is broken in the fall? Communion with God, specifically as children with their Father. Calvin emphasizes over and over again that humanity can no longer "from a mere survey of the world, infer that he is father."[13] In fact, worse—we now feel *terror* at the sight of God.[14] Whereas Adam was surrounded by signs of paternity that he can no longer discern, the future of humanity is to know God intimately as Father once again. Calvin sketches the story in broad brushstrokes familiar to us all: Adam refused to be the loving son, but a promise is given to his seed.[15] The story gains complexity as a new son is raised up through the seed of Abraham, and expands to include the nation of Israel, who is portrayed as this son. But here is a unique twist, particularly for one seen as a founder of the Protestant movement: Calvin emphasizes that Abraham was not justified by the promise or "a word," but "because he embraced God as his Father."[16] Even here, we find Calvin orienting that famous or (in)famous Protestant emphasis upon justification toward its ontological basis: communion.[17]

This, for Calvin, is the story of the Old Testament. It is the story of a Father who is trying to adopt his son, trying to bless his son, trying to protect his son. Calvin pays exquisite attention to the filial, father-child dimension found throughout the Old Testament because he believes that this is the pattern of God's communion with us. Even the cult and the law, those often opaque and downright difficult portions of Scripture to understand, receive this familial interpretation: they are to shape the people of God into sons. Calvin portrays the law

> *Calvin understands this primary relationship— that of Father and Son—to be at the root of all reality. We humans fit into this prior dynamic.*

not as the primary mode of relationship that God has with his people, but more like a "tutor" for a child, until the time "appointed by the father, after which [the child] enjoys his freedom."[18] The ceremonies are given the same treatment—they are "little external observances," akin to "rules for children's instruction"[19] that testify to the children that God alone can expiate guilt, forgive sin, and bring about communion. As Israel could not believe that God was a gracious Father, God had to institute a system to remind them of it![20] Through all of these strange and foreign and sometimes off-putting practices in the Old Testament, Calvin believes that God was attempting "to attest that he was Father, and to set apart for himself a chosen people."[21]

But the son (Israel) would have none of it. Calvin, through the mouth of Hosea, portrays the Father as lamenting the loss of communion with his children. "I have not otherwise governed them than as a father his own children; I have been bountiful towards them. I indeed wished to do them good, and, as it was right, required obedience from them."[22] It is in the framework of the faithful Father, and the wandering children, that Calvin most clearly articulates the work of Christ's salvation.

The Gospels: The Sonship of Christ

At last, in the fullness of time, God brings forth *the* Son.[23] Calvin writes, "Our Lord came forth as true man and took the person and the name of Adam in order to take Adam's place in obeying the Father."[24] The son in the garden failed; the son in the covenanted nation failed; but this Son does not fail. Here, at last, is a human fully in communion with God; here is a human rendering faithful filial obedience to the Father, and in their communion is our salvation. The quality of the life of Christ to which Calvin is most attuned is his lived Sonship—his life lived in listening and attentive fidelity to the Father. In places where the text does not even warrant it, Calvin interprets the primary dynamic as between Father and Son. In his baptism,

Calvin does not see Christ as fulfilling the law (as do his contemporaries), so much as rendering obedience to the Father. In his atoning sacrifice, Calvin says, "his willing obedience is the important thing."[25] Calvin even goes so far as to paint Christ as crying out, "Father, Father, why hast thou forsaken me?"—instead of the text's "my God, my God."[26] Pope John Paul II evokes the same truth (in *Dives in Misericordia*), when he writes that it is the "vision of the Father" that "constituted the central content of the messianic mission of the Son of Man."[27]

But Christ does not just do this *for* us, on our behalf. He invites us into this very relation—the communion of Father and Son. The filial story of God and humanity is not that of Adam—then Israel—and then Christ. It keeps going. It moves forward to *sons*. While Calvin acknowledges that terms like "father" and "son," when applied to humanity, are metaphors—anthropomorphisms—accommodated to our capacity to understand God's love for us, they are also more. "Here it is not a matter of figures … [rather, they are] founded upon the Head."[28] This particular metaphor flows from a reality that gives it substance: the Son, Jesus the Christ. "Christ has [no] thing, which may not be applied to our benefit,"[29] says Calvin—of which his Sonship is the supreme gift. This is no metaphor that humanity has projected onto God; it is God's own name for himself, given to man "to affect him inwardly."[30] (In fact, Calvin notes, fallen humanity is much more liable to project onto God negative, fearful images). "Therefore God both calls himself our Father and would have us so address him. By the great sweetness of this name he frees us from all distrust, since no greater feeling of love can be found elsewhere than in the Father."[31] From the hints and shadows of the Old Testament, God's people have been brought into to an unshakeable relationship of adoption by the Father. This has always been the momentum of the triune love.

Our Adoption into the Father-Son Relation

For Calvin, God becoming our Father is perhaps the best summary of the gospel.[32] He writes in his *Commentary on John*, "There are innumerable other ways, indeed, in which God daily testifies his fatherly love toward us, but the mark of adoption is justly preferred to them all."[33] Adoption reveals that it is not only the pardon, but the life of communion, that is now ours. For this, Calvin has no words—he gropes and fumbles, calling it the "mystical union," or, in shorthand, "our adoption." He writes, "We must understand that as long as Christ remains outside of us, and we are separated from him, all that he has done for the salvation of the human race remains useless and of no value for us. Therefore, to share with us what he has received from the Father, he had to become ours and to dwell within us."[34] And what is the primary thing that Christ has come to give to humanity? It is communion with his Father.

Calvin rarely, if ever, speaks of union with God. (Calvin notes that even Plato spoke eloquently of union with God). For Calvin, Christian union with God takes the shape of Christ: we are joined, by the Spirit, to Jesus who in turn *opens up to us his earthly relationship to his Father*. In union with Christ, Jesus's Father becomes our Father, we become children, and we enter the family dynamic. We move from being orphans to suddenly sitting around a table, eating the family food, being included in the Father's legacy, and getting in on everything in this family economy.[35]

If Christ's life on earth as the *Son* is the foundation for our adoption, then Calvin saw Christ's ascension as that which grounds our ongoing communion with the Father as the goal of the Christian life. Ascension is not so much that which establishes the physical church, but rather—with a human at the right hand of the Father—ascension is that which secures our future as communion with God. Ascent is primarily Christ's, yet his mission was to include us in his ascending return to the Father—for being with the Father is "the ultimate object at which you ought to aim."[36] Calvin is clear that Christ's descent to us would be cut short if it did not also result in our ascent with him, to communion with the Father. "Lift up your hearts" was Calvin's favorite saying of Origen, meaning the whole orientation of our heart, soul, and minds to communion with the Father, in the Son, by the Spirit.

So now we are ready to understand Calvin's particular understanding of communion: it has been flung open to us in Christ. Communion is not an amorphous quality of God, an anthropological tendency in humanity, or a mere counter to individualism. It has a peculiar shape—that of Father and Son. Just as Christ's whole identity was in the Father, so now our identity is found in the Son … and in his communion with the Father. It is perhaps for this reason that Calvin's pneumatology retained its non-instrumentalist flavor, for the Spirit is the one who brings the human into the heart of the Father-Son relation. Communion is entirely the domain of the Spirit, whose work is to bring us to live out of our new reality. Without the Spirit, Calvin says, "no one can taste either the fatherly favor of God or the beneficence of Christ."[37]

Because communion is the work of the Spirit, communion is not something we can manufacture, create, or manipulate. Neither Catholic synods nor Protestant potlucks can substitute for the Spirit's work to bring us into communion—a communion that is in Christ and one another. Communion is not something we can schedule or structure into the church. It is first and foremost our being brought, by the Spirit, into the Father-Son relation. We are invited into this living, trinitarian dynamic, this reality sketched out in John 13–17. And, living by the Spirit, out of our adoption, we then bring this reality to bear upon all of our life and relationships.

The Locus of Communion: The Church

Although it is only in Christ that we can come to know God as Father, for Calvin, there is no other place to know the Father than within the nurturing protection of our mother, the church. Calvin says in words very reminiscent of St. Cyprian that the church is the one "into whose bosom God is pleased to gather his sons."[38] And so it is not surprising that Calvin continues this familial imagery right into his discussion of the sacraments. If baptism is our "adoption," so the Eucharist is offered by a "provident householder" who supplies us with the food of life:[39]

> God has received us, once for all, into his family, to hold us not only as servants but as sons. Thereafter, to fulfill the duties of a most excellent Father concerned for his offspring, he undertakes also to nourish us throughout the course of our life.[40]

It is perhaps for this ecclesiological reason, and in language that makes some in the Catholic Church uncomfortable,[41] that Calvin resolutely refers to the Eucharist in the everyday, familial term of the "supper" or *la cène*.

In Christ, we enter our Sonship and our family. We are given our identity— we are not *in* Calvin, or *in* Francis, or *in* Augustine, but we are in the One in whom Calvin, Francis, Augustine found their identity: we are in Christ. It is this sonship-identity—this community with the Father and Son, by the Spirit—that grounds our communion with one another. Calvin asks, "What is the source of the *koinonia* or communion, which exists among us, but the fact that we are united to Christ so that we are 'flesh of his flesh, and bone of His bones?' For it is necessary for us to be incorporated, as it were, into Christ, in order to be united to each other."[42] Clearly, there is an order in Calvin's theology. First there is the trinitarian reality of communion, then there is the embodied reality. First there is our mystical union with Christ, as the *res* (the "thing"), and only then can there be the church—the physical expression of this communion.

So we find ourselves in the strange place of now approaching Calvin's eucharistic theology as both ordered to communion, and tempered by it. Calvin saw the life of Christ in three distinct phases: 1) Christ has gone before us—leading a life of communion with the Father, which 2) culminated in his ascension to the right hand of the Father; therefore 3) all the Christian life is to have this same momentum—toward being in Christ, who is in communion with the Father. It is the Eucharist that brings these three movements together. Calvin is adamant that the Lord's Supper is essential for our spiritual ascent of communion, speaking of it as "steps of a ladder."[43] This led to his famous metaphor that it is we who (in the Eucharist) must be "led up" to Christ (at the right hand of the Father), rather than "dragging him down" to our realm—which was Calvin's way of making communion the central miracle of the Supper. But does this not negate the reality of Christ's flesh and blood in our realm? How is it that Calvin can still insist that "it would be extreme madness to recognize no communion of believers with the flesh and blood of the Lord"?[44]

The ascension signaled to Calvin that the eucharistic question had to involve both substance and the Spirit. Just as Christ maintains his creaturely integrity as human at the right hand of the Father, so the bread and wine must be allowed to maintain their creaturely character as *meal* or "supper." And yet, as testimony to the work of the Spirit, these very elemental things are taken up, transfigured, brought nearer to their intended end by their participation in the Spirit. Calvin writes,

> It seems incredible that we should be nourished by Christ's flesh, which is at so great a distance from us. Let us bear in mind, that it is a secret and wonderful work of the Holy Spirit, which it were criminal to measure by the standard of our understanding. … Allow [Jesus] to remain in his heavenly glory, and aspire thou thither, that he may thence communicate himself to thee.[45]

The radical—even watershed—role that Calvin gave to the Spirit in the Lord's Supper cannot be overstated, for he (like the patristic fathers before him) attempted to take seriously the pneumatological dimensions of the presence of Christ. Just as it is the Spirit who brings us into Christ's relation to his Father, so it is the Spirit who brings humanity into the presence of Christ as the Eucharist is celebrated. The Eucharist is the locus of continuing *koinonia*, communion, with the Father and Son. As Calvin writes in a letter to a friend,

> For although the faithful come into this Communion [*koinonia*] on the very first day of their calling; nevertheless, inasmuch as the life of Christ increases in them, He daily offers Himself to be enjoyed by them. This is the Communion [*koinonia*] which they receive in the Sacred Supper.[46]

So according to this quotation, what do Christians receive in the Eucharist? They receive the very life of Christ—which they received on the first day of "their calling"—but which is an ongoing, ever-deepening reality. What they receive in the Supper, for Calvin, is no greater than, and certainly no less than, the miracle of being in communion with Christ, by the Spirit.

But here I must candidly admit that many strains within Protestantism do not reflect this strong sense of the presence of Christ in the bread and wine. The history of various Protestant denominations has perhaps borne out that it is difficult for us humans to begin "above" (with the spiritual, revealed reality) without being tempted to some strain of Gnosticism, in which the "below" (incarnate life on earth) is not in some way downgraded, or seen as unnecessary for one's private spiritual union. The natural link between the two is, of course, the person of the Spirit—which is why Calvin, though he can tread the line closely, never crosses it.[47] Yet, there is clearly strength to Calvin's structure: communion

is not limited to the institutional church. It is pre-eminently a reality within the Godhead itself, as revealed and flung open to us in the person of the Son. Church structures can bear testimony to this, and participate in it, by witnessing to it in the personal manner in which they conduct themselves.

The challenge to both Protestants and Catholics is the same—how do we live out of our communion with the Father, in the Son, by the Spirit? Is our identity secure in Christ—or is it in the structures of the church, or in some preferred theologian? Can we transform the impersonal structures of the church into a "school of communion" (as Pope John Paul II says, in *Novo Millennio Ineunte*), if we are not first participating in the source of communion itself? It is at this point that Calvin's gentle words are of utmost importance: this is the territory of the Spirit whose ongoing work is to draw us, and all of reality, into the uniqueness of the relation of the Father and Son. It is when we are in this unique relation that our own uniqueness is secured, and we can then and only then pour ourselves out for others. We must move from being individuals to becoming *persons*. It is ours to hear the Father calling us "beloved" in the desert of our identity, and from this place, to move forward into an identity as persons-in-communion, in Christ, in his body—the church. When we are living this communion, the church can then, as Pope John Paul II says, "reveal God, that Father, who allows us to 'see' Him in Christ."[48] ✗

Notes

1. Charles Taylor, *A Secular Age* (Cambridge: Harvard University Press, 2007), 753.

2. Ibid.

3. John Calvin, *A Reformation Debate: Sadoleto's Letter to the Genevans and Calvin's Reply*, ed. John C. Olin (New York: Harper & Row, 1966), 59.

4. Karl Barth, in a letter to Thurneysen, dated 8 June 1922 (*Revolutionary Theology in the Making: The Barth-Thurneysen Correspondence, 1914–1925* [London: Epworth, 1964], 101).

5. Karl Barth, *The Theology of the Reformed Confessions* (1923; repr., Philadelphia: Westminster John Knox, 2002), 94.

6. For a convincing argument to keep Calvin in the category of a "pre-modern" rather than "early mod-

ern" thinker, see Cornelis van der Kooi, *As in a Mirror: John Calvin and Karl Barth on Knowing God* (Leiden: Brill, 2005). The Enlightenment is far more profound a break than most care to account for when comparing Calvin to "modern" theologians.

7. All references to Calvin's *Institutes of the Christian Religion* are to the 1559 edition, unless noted. I am working from the two-volume Library of Christian Classics (20–21) edition, ed. John T. McNeil, trans. Ford Lewis Battles (Philadelphia: Westminster, 1960). This passage is from *Institutes* I.1.1, emphasis mine.

8. Ibid., II.6.1.

9. Ibid., I.13.21.

10. Calvin's *Commentary on Ephesians* 1:20. All references to Calvin's *Commentaries* are from the Calvin Translation Society (Edinburgh: 1843–55), reprinted by Baker, 1979.

11. T. F. Torrance, *The Trinitarian Faith* (Edinburgh: T&T Clark, 2000), 88, original emphasis.

12. *Institutes* I.14.2

13. Ibid., II.6.1

14. "But who might reach to him? Any one of Adam's children? No, like their father, all of them were terrified at the sight of God [Gen. 3:8]" (Ibid., II.12.1).

15. "For we must hold fast to that statement of St. Paul, that the blessing of Abraham was not promised to his seeds, but to his seed" (*Commentary on Exodus* 4:22).

16. *Commentary on Genesis* 15:16. This is no isolated case, for having embraced God as Father, Abraham is now the one with whom God enters into covenant—"and the adoption of his people was founded upon it" (*Commentary on Ezekiel* 16:8, Lecture 43). Circumcision, Calvin is quick to note, is Abraham's "pledge of adoption" (*Commentary on Genesis* 17:8).

17. In the 1999 *Joint Declaration on Justification*, we see that it is through the category of "love" (which is, of course, ordered to communion) that Lutheran and Catholic theologians approached a rapprochement over the subject.

18. *Commentary on Galatians* 4:1 "The pupil, although he is free and even lord of all his father's family, is still like a slave, for he is under the government of tutors. But this subjection under a guardian lasts only until the time appointed by the father, after which he enjoys his freedom. In this respect the fathers under the old covenant, being the sons of God, were free. But they were not in possession of freedom, since the law like a tutor kept them under its yoke. The slavery of the law lasted as long as God pleased and He put an end to it at the coming of Christ. Lawyers enumerate various methods by which guardianship is brought to a close; but of them all, the only one that fits this comparison is that which Paul puts here, the appointment by the father."

19. He continues, "until Christ should shine forth" (*Institutes* II.6.5).

20. Calvin's whole context of election keeps this from being an if/then conditional covenant. *Commentary on Genesis* 17:6, "see how kindly I indulge thee!"

21. *Institutes* II.9.1.

22. *Commentary on Hosea* 11:4.

23. Jesus is the true seed, *Institutes* II.6.2.

24. The quotation continues, "to present our flesh as the price of satisfaction to God's righteous judgment, and, in the same flesh, to pay the penalty that we had deserved" (Ibid., II.12.3).

25. Ibid., II.16.5.

26. *Institutes*, 1536, II.15 (Grand Rapids: Eerdmans, 1995).

27. *Dives in Misericordia*, 7.13.

28. "For here it is not a matter of figures, such as when atonement was set forth in the blood of beasts. Rather, they could not actually be sons of God unless their adoption was founded upon the Head" (*Institutes* II.14.5).

29. *Commentary on Hebrews* 7:25.

30. Van der Kooi, *As in a Mirror*, 188.

31. *Institutes* III.20.36.

32. "[Paul] proves that our salvation consists in having God as our Father" (*Commentary on Romans* 8:17).

33. *Commentary on John* 17:23.

34. *Institutes* III.1.1.

35. See in particular Calvin's expositions of the baptism of Christ. "It was rather the design of Christ to lay, as it were, in our bosom, a sure pledge of God's love toward us" (*Commentary on John* 15:9). This is explored in Julie Canlis, *Calvin's Ladder* (Grand Rapids: Eerdmans, 2010), 134–36.

36. *Commentary on John* 14:28.

37. *Institutes* III.1.2.

38. *Institutes* IV.1.1.

39. "For as in baptism, God, regenerating us, engrafts us into the society of his church and makes us his own by adoption, so we have said, that he discharges the function of a provident householder in continually supplying to us the food to sustain and preserve us in that life into which he has begotten us by his Word" (*Institutes* IV.1.1).

40. *Institutes* IV.17.1

41. "The term 'Lord's Supper' for the eucharist, then, is a complete novelty in Catholic tradition, and in liturgical history too. It would be better to talk about the eucharist as a fellowship, and about its ecclesial dimension, rather than to say that it has the character of a meal" (Walter Kaspar, *Theology and Church* [London: SCM, 1989], 189).

42. *Commentary 1 Corinthians* 10:16.

43. *Sermon II Samuel 6:1–7.*

44. *Institutes* IV.17.9.

45. *Commentary 1 Corinthians* 11:24.

46. Calvin, Letter to Peter Martyr, 8 August 1555.

47. For a fuller development of Calvin's doctrine of the Spirit, see Canlis, *Calvin's Ladder*, chap. 4.

48. *Dives in Misericordia*, 8.15.

Recovering the Person: The Crisis of Naturalism and the Theological Insights of Søren Kierkegaard and Karl Barth

Alan J. Torrance is Professor of Systematic Theology, University of St Andrews, and taught Regent summer courses over several years.

Andrew B. Torrance, Alan's son, is just completing a PhD on Kierkegaard and Barth at the University of Otago.

How does one begin to describe the person who is Jim Houston? First and foremost, he is one whose character has been defined in the most profound and radically integrated way by the good news from which he lives. He is a towering witness who has had the courage to "think big" and act accordingly in ways that are almost unparalleled in my experience. Without those qualities, we would not have, of course, Regent College and the unquantifiable contribution it has made to the theological and spiritual life of the church and, indeed, the academy—it is staggering to think of the number of academics alone whose vocation has been shaped by Regent!

One should not forget the courage it must have taken for Jim and Rita to desert the security and prestige of Oxford University and to take their family to Vancouver in pursuit of what must have seemed a risky and uncertain venture. It is rare for someone to totally change field midway through one's academic career. Not only did Jim become a theologian, but he became one with a remarkable knowledge of the history of ideas and one who has written extensively in biblical, pastoral, and spiritual theology.

This brings us to a further virtue: namely, his independence of mind and courage to move beyond the more sterile forms of theological engagement to pursue integrative and interdisciplinary research— all motivated, it should be emphasized, by his commitment to the gospel and the church's outreach. And what has never failed to inspire me, Alan, has been the integration of this theological and spiritual vision with a personal cheerfulness and joy in the faith even in the most difficult of circumstances. He has been the most profound witness to me personally in this regard.

Finally, his deep personal commitment to the well-being of persons from all walks of life and from diverse backgrounds is simply remarkable—and he treats all with an utterly genuine and overflowing Christian love. My father, James B. Torrance, who had the highest admiration for Jim, defines the Christian life as the gift of participating by the Spirit in the incarnate Son's communion with the Father and thereby in his mission to this broken world. Jim not only knows and understands that communion— intellectually and personally—but exhibits it and rejoices in it like no one else I have ever known. In so many ways, Jim defines what it is to be a person.

The purpose of this essay is to explore, albeit in a very limited way, the profound importance of the concept of the person not only for the well-being of the church, our society, and our culture, but also for the well-being of the academy that in so many ways and greatly to its detriment has lost sight of this massively significant element in the legacy of the Christian tradition.

This essay will be concerned to do two things. First, it seeks to outline the contemporary challenge faced by our culture and the academy that has resulted in the loss of the category of the person. Second, it seeks to respond to this challenge

Recovering the Person

CRUX: Fall 2012/Vol. 48, No. 3

by articulating, albeit briefly, the emphases that Christian theology must recover if it is to be an effective witness in the context of the threat to contemporary culture.

The Contemporary Challenge

The academic world faces an intellectual crisis. The so-called *universitas* is characterized by what Alvin Plantinga has shown to be two *mutually incompatible* methodologies and commitments. On the one hand, we have "naturalism," which is overwhelmingly dominant in the natural sciences. On the other, we have "Enlightenment humanism," or "creative anti-realism"[1]—what can also take the form of "social constructionism." This latter philosophy is incompatible with naturalism and sustains large areas of the humanities and the social sciences. Indeed, this family of philosophies is almost as influential in the humanities as naturalism is in the sciences. It is found in history, literary studies, film studies, continental philosophy, gender studies, religious studies, and various other departments within the "social sciences." Unfortunately, like most contagions, it is also flourishing in theology departments![2] What this kind of approach does is place the subjective human thinker at the centre of the universe—whereby the human subject creates not only the sphere of meaning, but also of value and even truth. Richard Rorty, arguably the father of postmodern philosophy, suggests that the truth is "what our peers will, *ceteris paribus* [other things being equal], let us get away with saying."[3] The impact of this on thinking about the person is clear. It evacuates the self from a moral universe and enthrones the human subject as the source of all truth, value, and meaning. Rather than elevating the person, as it appears to do, it ultimately demeans the person by reducing the grounds of the person's dignity to a nihilistic arbitrariness.

In radical (if superficial) contradistinction to Enlightenment humanism, philosophical naturalism regards the human person as all but insignificant in the grand scheme of things. It is the contemporary

challenge of naturalism that we wish to engage primarily in this essay. What is naturalism? Roger Trigg defines it as the view that "reality is wholly accessible (at least in principle) to the natural sciences. Nothing … can exist beyond their reach."[4] Plantinga defines it as the view that "there is no God, and we human beings are insignificant parts of a giant cosmic machine that proceeds in majestic indifference to us, our hopes and aspirations, our needs and desires, our sense of fairness, or fittingness."[5] We see this in Richard Dawkins's vision of reality when he writes, "The universe we observe has precisely the properties we should expect if there is, at bottom, no design, no purpose, no evil and no good, nothing but blind, pitiless indifference."[6] We are the products of a "blind watchmaker."[7] As George Gaylord Simpson puts it, "Man is the result of a purposeless and natural process that did not have him in mind."[8]

Although there is nothing new about naturalism per se—it is as old as Lucretius—it has become the standard reductionist assumption of research in the biological sciences, anthropology, sociobiology, and the cognitive sciences. Its effect is a radical devaluing of all that we associate with the world of the personal. As Plantinga points out, it anaesthetizes society and the academy against the notion of an objective sphere of value,[9] as also of human rights and human dignity. Ultimately, moreover, it undermines the virtues of truthfulness and academic integrity.[10]

How should we respond? First, we must repudiate the rhetorical assumption, rampant throughout the writings of our "four horsemen" of contemporary atheism (Harris, Dennett, Dawkins, and Hitchens), that the forces of reason are on the side of "scientific naturalism" and against theism. Ironically, few do that more effectively than the leading atheist philosopher Quentin Smith, who, until recently, was editor of *Philo*, the journal of the Society of Humanist Philosophers—whose editorial board reads like the "who's who" of modern atheism and includes Daniel

Dennett, Richard Gale, John Searle, J.J.C. Smart, and so on. In 2001, Smith wrote a lengthy editorial article entitled "The Metaphilosophy of Naturalism." After arguing that whereas thirty years ago theism was devoid of academic credibility, now "one-quarter to one-third of philosophy professors are theists, with most being orthodox Christians." He concludes, "God is not 'dead' in academia."[11] Referring to the "erudite brilliance of theistic philosophizing today," he then suggests that theistic argumentation has become so impressive that if a group of naturalists and theists were locked in a room together, and a naturalist were appointed to referee the ensuing debates, the "most probable outcome is that the naturalist, wanting to be a fair and objective referee, would have to conclude that the theists definitely had the upper hand in every single argument or debate."[12] He concludes,

> The vast majority of naturalist philosophers have come to hold (since the late 1960s) an unjustified belief in naturalism. Their justifications have been defeated by arguments developed by theistic philosophers, and now naturalist philosophers, for the most part, live in darkness about the justification of naturalism. ... If naturalism is true, then their belief in naturalism is *accidentally true*.[13]

It is worth comparing Quentin Smith's honest representation of the place of theistic explanation in the academy with Daniel Dennett's derisory references to theism as naive self-deceit:

> The kindly God who lovingly fashioned each and every one of us and sprinkled the sky with shining stars for our delight—that God is, like Santa Claus, a myth of childhood, not anything a sane, undeluded adult could literally believe in. That God must either be turned into a symbol for something less concrete or abandoned altogether.[14]

In the light of Quentin Smith's statements, we can conclude that when Richard Dawkins comments in *The Blind Watchmaker* that "Darwin made it possible to be an intellectually fulfilled atheist," his optimism constitutes nothing short of "Santa Claus atheism"; that is, a flagrant example of naturalistic wishful thinking.[15]

This philosophy, which characterizes the assumptions of the vast majority of the biological sciences, is driven not by science but by a myth. Metaphysical naturalism sees human beings as insignificant parts of an impersonal, cosmic machine that is essentially amoral and in which value judgements are devoid of reference as are the claimed "academic values" of truth, intellectual integrity, and moral responsibility integral to the proper function of the scientific community. For Patricia Churchland, human beings are nothing more than "nervous systems" caught up in the evolutionary derby that is driven by what she famously refers to as the four F's: feeding, fleeing, fighting, and reproducing. All that we are is a product of whatever it is that "*enhances the organism's chances of survival.*" She then ends, "Truth, *whatever that is*, definitely takes the hindmost."[16] To reiterate, what should be clear is that this myth serves to undermine the very values that define the academic enterprise and without which it could not function at all—namely, the pursuit of "truth" and the concepts of intellectual and ethical accountability that attend this.

Trinitarian Theism

The above discussion has sought to do two things. First, it has sought to expose the fact that by displacing the Christian legacy of the concept of the person, metaphysical naturalism jeopardizes the whole system of values (intellectual and otherwise) on which the proper functioning of both the contemporary academy and our contemporary culture are grounded. Second, it has sought to establish that, although there was a time when theism had "such a low epistemic status that it did not meet the standards of an 'academically respectable' position to hold," this is emphatically no longer the case in the academy—something that our all-too-influential "four horsemen" have chosen to ignore.[17] What Christian theism provides us with is critical explanatory power at precisely the points where naturalism is embarrassingly devoid of it. Theism explains "why there is something rather than nothing."[18] That is, it explains why the natural sciences have something with which to engage. It explains the intelligibility of the contingent order—that is, why it is possible for the human mind to penetrate its workings and operations. These things are presupposed by all scientific inquiry and yet are not things that science could ever be in a position to explain. Theism explains the staggering degree of fine-tuning of the universe without which there would be no intelligent life whatsoever. Further, it attests to the existence of a moral universe and the system of values—that is, truth, honesty, transparency, and accountability in research—that are presupposed by the proper function of the scientific enterprise. In sum, science assumes the capacity and conditions of personal knowledge, and it is the category of the *personal*, integral to this, that is arguably the most significant legacy to the academy of Christian theism.

It is imperative, however, that we do not make the mistake of assuming that general arguments for the cogency and coherence of theism will establish a religious viewpoint that will thereby affirm the category of the person. Christians are not characterized by holding a general and amorphous belief in God. Indeed, they are not to be perceived as opting for a general belief in God and then opting for belief in the Christian God. Christians are "theists" because the Triune God has revealed himself to them in a reconciling act—bringing them through the Spirit to participate in the risen life of the incarnate Lord and in his communion with the Father.

It is precisely here that we stand to benefit from the profound insights of Søren Kierkegaard and Karl Barth for articulating the unique and specific character of Christian theism—and the extent to which natural theological arguments for theism in general, though not to be dismissed a priori as false, should *not* be regarded as underpinning, in any way, Christian conversion. Both Kierkegaard and Barth see Christian faith as the result of an unanticipatable, creative, and reconciling event of free divine agency whereby actual persons are brought to concrete faith in Jesus Christ—a faith that involves the transformed interpretation of every facet of existence. It is not to be seen as developing out of (or as an outward expression of) that which is immanent within our thinking and reasoning. Rather, it is the consequence of our being "metamorphosed" for the sake of the discernment of truth and no longer "schematized" by the secular order, to use the language Paul adopts in Romans 12:2.

The Decisiveness of the Historical

Whereas theism-in-general denotes belief, by means of a kind of intellectual *ascent*, in the existence of the transcendent God, Christian faith denotes the recognition of the God who *descends* to meet us personally and in person. The recognition that God enters into our situation to encounter us in history means that historical events constitute the *sine qua non* of Christian theism. Thus, the central question that the Christian theologian is required to address (and that established religion too often avoids) is whether the historical is of *decisive* as opposed to merely *illustrative* significance. Arguably, no thinker has addressed this question more significantly since Athanasius than Søren Kierkegaard. In *Philosophical Fragments*, Kierkegaard sets out to expose the implications of interpreting Christian experience from an idealist perspective[19] through his non-Christian pseudonym, Johannes Climacus.[20] To do this, he begins by providing an account of the Socratic approach.

According to the Socratic account, human beings can only recognize the truth to the extent that the truth is already inherent, even if dormant, in the mind. We can only *recognize* the truth if we already know it. It is, moreover, these universal truths that matter and that must not be confused with the particular, which is insignificant or, at best, merely illustrative. The particular moment when an individual discovers the truth and the particular teacher who prompts an individual to recollect the truth are of no real significance, on a Socratic account: "Viewed socratically, any point of departure in time is *eo ipso* [of itself] something accidental, a vanishing, an occasion. Nor is the teacher anything more."[21] For Socrates, the truth resides in the mind; it cannot enter into the mind, and no condition can be gained that leads the mind to discover something new or outside the mind. All that a learner needs to realize the truth is a "socratic midwife": a teacher who can jog the mind or "bring to birth" what is immanently there.[22] Again, the particular identity of the midwife is necessarily irrelevant to the learner's relation to the truth.

After briefly setting out some of the key features of the Socratic approach, just mentioned, Climacus goes on to consider the possibility of an alternative way of attaining the truth:[23] "If the situation is to be different, then the moment in time must be of decisive significance."[24] If a moment in history is to be decisive to an individual's capacity to access the truth, Climacus supposes, "the seeker up until that moment must not have possessed the truth. ... Consequently, he has to be defined as being outside the truth."[25] Therefore, the learner would be in a state of untruth. This condition would enslave the mind in untruth, keeping it captive until a new condition could be achieved that would liberate the mind from the alienated forms of thought that conditioned its thinking. For the mind to be set free to learn the truth, he suggests, the learner would require much more than a mere midwife

to prompt the learner into recollecting the truth. The learner would need someone that could "provide him with the condition for understanding it." This person, then, must have the ability to transform the learner, an ability that far surpasses the powers of a mere human teacher: "no human being is capable of doing this; if it is to take place, it must be done by the god himself."[26]

What Kierkegaard accomplishes here, through Climacus, is to show us the coherence of an alternative way of understanding how persons might relate to the truth—an alternative that is analogous to the gospel message. Through this account, Kierkegaard questions the unyielding confidence in the powers of immanent human reason and opens the doors to the suggestion that the truth is to be found through a faithful relationship with the God who is *beyond* human reason—and who is not conjured up from the mind's own resources by philosophical argumentation or analysis. In presenting us with this, Kierkegaard draws attention to the gospel truth that God can only be known in and through a relationship with the God who discloses himself to us *personally* in history—in Jesus Christ who is the way, the truth, and the life. For Kierkegaard, it is by encountering God in the presence of the "God in time" that our minds are delivered from error and reconciled to the truth, enabling us to discern the true reality for which we were created—a discernment that takes place *before God*. As Kierkegaard affirms, through Climacus, faithful theology must reject any attempt to operate with an account of an "immanental underlying kinship between the temporal and the eternal, because the eternal itself has entered into time and wants to establish kinship there."[27]

The whole shape of Barth's approach parallels these same emphases. Barth is not interested in what is possible theologically, with what can (or cannot) be established about God a priori by "natural" theological means. Rather, he is concerned that theology be *obedient*. For Barth, the Christian life is a *Christ*-ian life for which God creates us and into which God reconciles us—"under God and in accord with God."[28] What distinguishes the Reformed Barth from the Lutheran Kierkegaard, however, is the more Trinitarian emphasis we find in Barth's account of revelation—rather than the primarily christocentric emphasis we see in Kierkegaard. Whereas, for Kierkegaard, revelation primarily concerns God becoming human in Christ, Barth shows much more of an appreciation for its trinitarian form, recognizing the Father, Son, and Spirit as "Revealer, Revelation and Revealedness [or being revealed]."[29] For Barth, the Triune God "reveals Himself *through Himself*."[30] At the same time, his arguments echo Kierkegaard's in affirming that God and God's active presence are the reconciling conditions for knowing God. The condition is emphatically not to be conceived in terms of some immanent capacity within the self.

The Infinite Qualitative Difference

In an oft-quoted statement, Barth comments, "If I have a system, it is limited to a recognition of what Kierkegaard called the 'infinite qualitative distinction' between time and eternity": "God is in heaven, and thou art on earth."[31] There is, in short, no human system for understanding the relationship between God and humanity—other than a system that acknowledges our inherent inability to develop such a system. Metaphorically, just as we cannot describe smells with colours, we cannot describe the real God with human words and qualifications—there is an explanatory gap. The basis of this gap lies in the fact that God can only be known in the presence of his free activity—in the presence of his grace. This is because the God of the Christian faith, the God who becomes one with us in history, in Jesus of Nazareth, is the *real* God who is neither immediately nor immanently *knowable* in this finite and fallen world—he can neither be directly observed nor stumbled upon by the human imagination.[32] God is known by being actually and concretely present to humanity, engaging with us in ways that reconcile our alienated minds and deliver us from our dysfunctional perception of reality.

For both Kierkegaard and Barth, the central reason for stressing the infinite qualitative difference is to draw our attention away from our own static human ideas and ideals toward God's personal and dynamic engagement with us as the historical Jesus Christ. This is not to suggest that the incarnation deletes the infinite qualitative difference between humanity and God. Rather, Jesus Christ draws us, by the Spirit, into a life of faithful fellowship with the Father, creating real yet mediated communion between human beings and God despite the infinite qualitative difference. It is precisely in and through this event of reconciling self-disclosure that God bestows personhood on human creatures, creating, thereby, a new humanity who are defined in and through participation in the *eschatos Adam*, the true *imago Dei*, the sole *imago patris*. In sum, it is in and through our being drawn to participate in Christ that we are constituted "from above" as *persons* in truth—an event in which, as John Zizioulas has argued so powerfully, we find our being as an event of communion.

Truth and Subjectivity

Kierkegaard's account of the Christian faith interprets any suggestion that "I live" the Christian life as requiring to be qualified retrospectively by the statement "yet not I but Christ in me."[33] The reason for this is that, for Kierkegaard, we cannot stand apart from our own subjective lives in order to confirm how Jesus Christ is working in our lives and drawing us into a life of faith. That this is indeed what is happening is known by no other means than by faith itself. In short, to believe this is to recognize that we believe this by the grace of God, through a relationship with Jesus Christ. In acknowledging this, the Christian is affirming that her faith in the reality of God is not simply a product of her own belief-forming imagination but is always grounded in the reality of Jesus Christ.[34] To be related

CRUX: Fall 2012/Vol. 48, No. 3

to Jesus Christ as "the way and the truth and the life" is to live in the light of that which lies beyond human subjectivity. Unless we live from that centre in history that is Jesus Christ, we are left helplessly living from beliefs that are not merely unchristian but also untrue.

With this in mind, Kierkegaard (or, more accurately, Johannes Climacus) argues that "subjectivity is untruth." His point is that the truth to which we are referring here is not something that we can *possess* subjectively. For Kierkegaard, as also for Barth, to be in relation to the Truth is to be in relation to a *person*, Jesus Christ, who radically transcends immanent human thought or any subjective system of ideas. Thus, for both thinkers, becoming a Christian does not merely involve the transformation of our knowing but involves our reconciliation into a relationship with the truth; that is, into a relationship with the objective God. This means that becoming a Christian is not grounded in a person's relationship to God per se but rather in God's active relationship to that person, realized in the presence of Jesus Christ through the power of the Holy Spirit. Thus, for Barth, "theology is concerned, not with the encounter between nature and supernature, but with the encounter between nature and grace, or concretely, with the encounter between man and the Word of God."[35] Again, in this dynamic we do not have two realities engaging with one another "as though they are on the same plane, as though there can be between them co-ordination, continuity or interchange, or as though in the last resort they are somehow identical."[36]

> *Our personhood is defined according to the purposes of the Triune Creator, and is realized for us by this same Creator becoming human and reconciling us into a life of participation within the triune koinonia.*

God and humanity can only correspond with one another through a relationship of "receptivity and spontaneity, gift and demand."[37] And this is only possible because of the mediation of the God-human, Jesus Christ. As Kierkegaard (or, more accurately, his Christian pseudonym, Anti-Climacus) puts it,

> That the human race is supposed to be in kinship with God is ancient paganism; but *that* an individual human being is God is Christianity, and this particular human being is the God-man.[38]

For Barth, this means that

> Christians are found only in Christ, not independently. They are seen only from above, not from below, only by faith, not by sight. They do not exist, therefore, as do Mohammedans, Buddhists, atheists, Catholics or Protestants.[39]

The implications are clear. For both Kierkegaard and Barth, it is Jesus Christ who defines our personhood. Consequently, the Christian vision of the person is grounded exclusively in the reconciliation that has taken place in Immanuel, God with us. This means that our personhood does not repose on the activity of our fragile and capricious minds but on the Triune God who is beyond our minds and the fellowship generated by the Holy Spirit. In short, it is the reconciling mission of the Triune God that both humanizes and personalizes us in and through the creative presence of the Spirit of Christ that does not merely personalize us as individuals, but personalizes as in and through participation in the life of the body of Christ.

What this Christian worldview tells us is that communion is not to be viewed as a social construct. Personhood is neither something we accomplish nor achieve, as Enlightenment humanism might suggest. Nor is it bestowed on us by the (impersonal) laws of nature, as the metaphysical naturalist might suggest. Rather, our personhood is defined according to the purposes of the Triune Creator, and is realized for us by this same Creator becoming human and reconciling us into a life of participation within the triune *koinonia*.

What is pastorally so significant is the unity that this proclaims within creation. It can only be by recourse to the purposes of the one eternal Creator, who becomes human, that there can be any talk of a world united in one universal purpose. By taking this point seriously, we are provided with an account of the person that, given its one uniting foundation, holds forth an "inclusive" vision that transcends the irreducibly diverse perspectives of individual human beings. What this suggests is that we are only properly functional when we are united by a single all embracing purpose; that is, when society takes the form of the body of Christ, as the community who participates in the triune life of God. Further, this suggests that all polarization and oppression constitute, in essence, a failure to understand the ontology of the person.

The socio-political significance, therefore, of this vision of the person reposes on a form of the *analogia communionis*:

as the Father is to the Son in the Spirit:
so the incarnate Son is to the Body of
    Christ in that same Spirit:
so the Body of Christ is to the secular
    culture, through that same
    Spirit.

To recapitulate, the definition of the Christian life is the gift of participation by the Spirit in the incarnate Son's communion with the Father and in the Father's mission to the world, in the Son and through the Spirit. It is that same mission that calls the church to a ministry of reconciliation whereby an alienated humanity might be "metamorphosed" and no longer "schematized" by the secular order for the sake of the discernment of truth—a discernment fundamental to which is the recognition of what it means to be created a person.

Never has this been more relevant than in an age in which the dual philosophies of metaphysical naturalism and Enlightenment humanism have sought to rob the academy of that vision of the person that has been Christianity's most significant legacy to society and, indeed, the academy. It is still more relevant when digital media serve to commodify every facet of human existence resulting in what is now being widely described as an irreversible pornographization of the younger generation in ways that undermine properly functional personal relationships—and, as neuroscientists are suggesting, the brain function that is the correlate of these.

This development is indicative of a culture increasingly tempered by the philosophies of metaphysical naturalism and Enlightenment humanism. On the one hand, the subliminal impact of a naturalistic mindset too easily gives rise to the politics of unfettered exploitation and die-hard nationalism. On the other hand, the postmodern evisceration of the language of accountability elevates human autonomy to a point where the unrestricted exercise of our freedoms is our "right" and exploitative pornography and gratuitous violence become the new art forms of a digital age.

Witnessing the moral disintegration of Germany under the demonic tyranny of National Socialism, Karl Barth stressed the primacy of confession over moral condemnation and that our focus must be on God's "Yes" to humanity in Jesus Christ. The primary affirmation of the Barmen Declaration reads as follows: "Jesus Christ, as he is attested to us in Holy Scripture, is the one Word of God whom we have to hear, and whom we have to trust and obey in life and in death." What he saw is as true today as it was then; namely, that the church is never more relevant than when it has the courage simply to be the body of Christ. Only then can the world glimpse what it means to be human in truth and, more specifically, what it means to be a person. It is only when the world discovers what it means to have one's being in communion that it acquires the condition to recognize the underlying form of its folly. And it is only when it is given to share in the triune life of the One through whom and for whom all things were created that it will find the fulfillment and shalom that it subliminally craves. ✗

Notes

1. In this section we are summarizing Alvin Plantinga's analysis, which can be found in his Stob Lectures, entitled "The Twin Pillars of Christian Scholarship," published *The Twin Pillars of Christian Scholarship* (Grand Rapids, MI: Calvin College and Seminary, 1990). See also his essay, "Advice to Christian Philosophers," *Faith and Philosophy* 1, no. 3 (1984), 253–71. A related discussion of naturalism is found in Alan J. Torrance, "Is There a Distinctive Human Nature? Approaching the Question from a Christian Epistemic Base," to be published in *Zygon*, December 2012.

2. This is evident in much of Gordon Kaufman's work, but its *reductio ad absurdum* is to be found in the writings of Don Cupitt and Lloyd Geering.

3. Richard Rorty, *Philosophy and the Mirror of Nature* (Princeton: Princeton University Press, 1980), 176.

4. Roger Trigg, *Philosophy Matters* (Malden, MA: Blackwell, 2001), 149.

5. Plantinga, *Twin Pillars*, 9–10.

6. Richard Dawkins, *River Out of Eden* (London: Weidenfeld & Nicholson, 1995), 133.

7. "All appearances to the contrary, the only watchmaker in nature is the blind forces of physics, albeit deployed in a very special way. A true watchmaker has foresight: he designs his cogs and springs, and plans their interconnections, with a future purpose in his mind's eye. Natural selection, the blind, unconscious automatic process which Darwin discovered, and which we now know is the explanation for the existence and apparently purposeful form of all life, has no purpose in mind. It has no mind and no mind's eye. It does not plan for the future. It has no vision, no foresight, no sight at all. If it can be said to play the role of watchmaker in nature, it is the blind watchmaker." Richard Dawkins, *The Blind Watchmaker* (New York: Norton, 1986), 5.

8. George Gaylord Simpson, *The Meaning of Evolution*, rev. ed. (New Haven: Yale University Press, 1967), 345.

9. In *Warranted Christian Belief* (New York: Oxford University Press, 2000) Plantinga discusses Herbert Simon's analysis of altruism in an article entitled "A Mechanism for Social Selection and Successful Altruism," *Science* 250 (December, 1990), 1665–68. One of the puzzles that Simon (a leading academic cognitive scientist, expert in cybernetics and winner of a Nobel Prize in economic science) sought to address is why certain people do not behave in the ways in which evolutionary theory would dictate; that is, the effective spreading of one's genes. How, for example, do we explain the Mother Theresas of this world? His answer is framed in terms of two principles; namely, a) docility—some people are docile and tend to do what they are encouraged to do (that is, they do what their peers tell them to do without adequately questioning it!); and b) limited rationality, or, as Plantinga explains "stupidity" (214n21). In terms of his naturalistic account, therefore, morally virtuous or self-denying people like Mother Theresa are an unhappy quirk of fate. Happily, their insufficiently evolved and evolving genes will be condemned by the evolutionary process, and the docile gullibility and stupidity constitutive of their altruism purified from the gene pool!

10. Cf. Alvin Plantinga, *The Twin Pillars of Christian Scholarship*, The Stob Lectures of Calvin College and Seminary, booklet published by Calvin College, Grand Rapids, MI, 1989, 9–17.

11. Quentin Smith, "The Metaphilosophy of Naturalism," *Philo* 4, no. 2 (2001): 3.

12. Ibid., 5.

13. Ibid. (emphasis original).

14. Richard Dawkins, *Darwin's Dangerous Idea: Evolution and the Meanings of Life* (London: Penguin, 1996), 18.

15. Dawkins, *Blind Watchmaker*, 6.

16. Patricia Churchland, "Epistemology in the Age of Neuroscience," *Journal of Philosophy* 84, no. 10 (October 1987): 548 (emphasis original).

17. Smith, "Metaphilosophy of Naturalism," 3.

18. Strictly speaking, this traditional way of formulating the question addressed by the cosmological argument is mistaken as there is no logical possibility of there being "nothing" if God is a necessary being!

19. Idealists believe that objects of knowledge are dependent on the activity of the human mind: we can only discover the truth because it is already immanent within the human mind.

20. It is significant to Kierkegaard's argument that his pseudonym is non-Christian. It enables him to say that you don't have to be a Christian to perceive the radical and irreducible incompatibility between idealism and Christianity.

21. Søren Kierkegaard, *Philosophical Fragments*, ed. and trans. Howard V. Hong and Edna H. Hong (Princeton: Princeton University Press, 1985), 11.

22. Ibid., 9–13.

23. As the Hongs point out, "No distinction is made here between Socrates and Plato. Nor is a distinction made in *Fragments* between Socrates-Plato and philosophical idealism nor between them and naturalism and scientific humanism, inasmuch as all of them presuppose an immanental possession of genuine knowledge or of the condition for acquiring it" (*Philosophical Fragments*, 277n8).

24. *Philosophical Fragments*, 13. Under the influence of Kierkegaard, Barth also draws attention to the importance of the "moment" (*Augenblick*) in his second volume of *Romans*. For a few examples, see Karl Barth, *The Epistle to the Romans*, trans. Edwyn C. Hoskyns (London: Oxford University Press, 1933), 109–12, 116, 124, 137, 166, 188, 227, 336, 497–98; vol. 2, 83–86, 91, 99, 114, 143, 167, 209, 481–82.

25. *Philosophical Fragments*, 13.

26. Ibid., 14–15.

27. Søren Kiekregaard, *Concluding Unscientific Postscript to Philosophical Fragments*, ed. and trans. Howard V. Hong and Edna H. Hong (Princeton: Princeton University Press, 1992), 573.

28. Karl Barth and Eduard Thurneysen, *Revolutionary Theology in the Making: Barth-Thurneysen Correspondence, 1914–1925*, trans. James D. Smart (Richmond: Westminster John Knox, 1964), 83.

29. *The Doctrine of the Word of God*, 2nd ed., ed. G. W. Bromiley and T. F. Torrance, vol. 2, pt. 2 of *Church Dogmatics* (Edinburgh: T&T Clark, 1975), 295, 314 (hereafter *CD* I/1). Barth also writes, "It is God Himself, it is the same God in unimpaired unity, who according to the biblical understanding of revelation is the revealing God and the event of revelation and its effect on man" (*CD* I/1, 299).

30. *CD* I/1, 296.

31. Written in the preface to the second edition of Barth's *Epistle to the Romans*, trans. Edwyn C. Hoskyns (London: Oxford University Press, 1933), 10.

32. As T. F. Torrance notes, Barth was deeply indebted "to Kierkegaard's attack upon all direct communication" (*Karl Barth: An Introduction to His Early Theology, 1910–31* [London: SCM, 1962], 44). While Torrance makes a fair point here, it is an overstatement for him to say previously that "Theologically and philosophically it was undoubtedly Kierkegaard who had the greatest impact upon him [Barth], far greater than the actual mentioning of his name, in the *Romans*, for example, indicates" (44).

33. We are alluding to an archaic translation of Gal. 2:20, which the NRSV translates, "it is no longer I who live, but it is Christ who lives in me."

34. Struggling with this paradox himself, Kierkegaard writes in a journal entry, "If I consider my own personal life, am I then a Christian or is my personal life purely a poet-existence, even with an addition of something demonic ... perhaps, for perhaps it would nevertheless turn out that I would not become a Christian." *Journals and Papers: Autobiographical 1848–1855*, ed. and trans. Howard V. Hong and Edna H. Hong (Bloomington: Indiana University Press, 1978), 6431.

35. *CD* I/2, 791.

36. Ibid., 790–91.

37. Ibid., 791.

38. *Practice in Christianity*, ed. and trans. Howard V. Hong and Edna H. Hong (Princeton: Princeton University Press, 1991), 82 (emphasis original).

39. *CD* I/2, 790–91.

Amani ya Juu ("A Higher Peace"): African Refugee Women Living Out Reconciliation in Nairobi

Diane Stinton

Diane Stinton is the Dean of Students and Associate Professor of Mission Studies at Regent College.

Author's Note: This article is largely based on a chapter titled "Amani ya Juu ('Peace from Above'): African Women Refugees Living Out Reconciliation in Nairobi" in Religion and Politics in East Africa: Reflections for Theology in the 21st Century, The Ecumenical Symposium of Eastern Africa Theologians (ESEAT) series, ed. Peter Kanyandago and Diane Stinton (Nairobi: Paulines Publications Africa, 2008), 124–42.

Cardinal to James Houston's thought is the theme of reconciliation in Christ. Indeed, the very heart of spiritual life is discovering and living out this reconciliation in every dimension of life—with God, with oneself, with others, and with all of creation.

Having been nurtured by Jim Houston's teaching and mentoring in spiritual theology, I have sought to discern glimpses of reconciliation throughout several years of ministry in Nairobi, Kenya. Within the context of East Africa, where violence is rife at many levels—political, ethnic, domestic, and personal—I came to appreciate a Swahili proverb: "When elephants fight the grass gets trampled."[1] Without a doubt, among those who are most "trampled" in the "elephant" conflicts across Africa are refugees, approximately 50 percent of whom are women and girls especially susceptible to all kinds of human rights abuses. Their plight validates a key observation of theologian Robert Schreiter, who contends that "men are most frequently the source of the violence that rends families, communities, and nations apart," and that "it is often left to women to find ways of repairing the damage that men's violence and conflict have wrought."[2] Citing examples from around the world of how women have intervened, sometimes in dramatic ways, to break deadlocks of conflict, Schreiter underlines

the pivotal role women play in suffering, violence, and reconciliation. They are frequently the victims. ... They are the ones who survive. And they are the ones who find a non-violent way out of violent situations. They teach others how to cope, to heal memories, and to move on.[3]

If this be the case, are there any indications within East Africa of refugee women playing such a pivotal role in moving on from violent conflicts toward healing and reconciliation? This article explores the theme of reconciliation through a case study of one particular community of refugee women in Nairobi: *Amani ya Juu*. The name, translated from Swahili as "a higher peace" or "peace from above," intimates that the source of the peace and reconciliation these women seek lies beyond human means alone. Their fundamental commitment to drawing upon spiritual sources and strategies is in line with John Mbiti's assertion that "religion can contribute more to peace and reconciliation than either political measure or cultural activities—however important and necessary these are."[4] Consequently, this article examines concepts of reconciliation that emerge in the interface of African indigenous religion and Christianity, and how this dual heritage of African and biblical tradition shapes contemporary practices of peace and reconciliation. Following brief synopses of reconciliation within these religious traditions, the case study will focus on how it is being lived out in creative ways within this one community of refugee women in Nairobi today. In particular, the women's own perceptions are crucial, for they allow insight into what Schreiter terms "the spirituality of reconciliation: how reconciliation is experienced, how that experience can become a key to a new way of living, and how that living might be shared with and transmitted to others."[5]

Reconciliation in Indigenous African Thought

There is no single concept of reconciliation among human societies, for each culture determines what it means and what it entails. Certainly reconciliation holds a predominant place in indigenous African thought, for it is critical in seeking and maintaining the very social harmony that is fundamental to African religions. For example, Laurenti Magesa notes that "in fact, reconciliation (*kutasa*) penetrates practically the entire religious system (*butasi*) of the Taita" people of Kenya.[6] The central purpose of this particular religion is said to be the restoration of "*sere*: peace, health and general well-being."[7] The only way to restore and retain the desired relationships is to get rid of the anger that arises within humans, domestic animals, and spiritual powers, and this is accomplished primarily through ritual means. Significantly, as the one performing the ritual, the human agent's own heart must be free from anger:

> In *kutasa* [reconciliation], … the Taita held that for the entire ritual to be efficacious, it was necessary for the celebrant to be "sincere": he must not have inner reservations. Although the performance of *kutasa* was correctly achieved in gesture and word, these had to be matched by the person's inner state.[8]

Thus there are two dimensions to reconciliation: seeking external harmony with other community members wherever relationships have been disrupted, and also the inner peace that is prerequisite for doing so.[9]

These two dimensions of reconciliation, the external and the internal, are addressed in African religions through various means. One major way is through prayer, as Mbiti illustrates through citing various prayers of African peoples, including the following from the Wapokomo people of Kenya:

> O God, give us peace, give us tranquillity, and let good fortune come to us. … O God, give us rain, we are in misery we suffer with our sons. Send us the clouds that bring the rain. … Let her who is sick, O God, receive from thee health and peace, and her village and her children and her husband. Let her get up and go to work, let her work in the kitchen, let her find peace again.[10]

As Mbiti observes, this prayer reveals the Wapokomo people's conviction that God is the giver of peace, and that peace comes as a gift of God to the whole world including people and nature. Indeed, one expression of peace from God is the ongoing provision of rain that sustains life. Mbiti explains, "Water is the most explicit symbol of life. Life and peace go hand in hand. Where there is peace, there is abundance of life. The absence of peace is a threat to life, a diminution of life, a destruction of life; it is suffering leading to annihilation."[11] Moreover, the prayer reflects how peace is viewed in terms of "tranquillity," "good fortune," "good health," and "freedom to live and to work." Finally, peace is considered to have both communal and individual dimensions: rain is certainly a gift for the whole community, yet the personal aspect of peace is conveyed as well. Mbiti summarizes:

> The restoration of health is petitioned for a sick woman, her village, her children and her husband. … Where there is no peace, there is suffering for the individual and for the wider

community—children, husband, wife, family, village, neighbours, clan, society and the environment (nature).[12]

A second major way of enacting peace and reconciliation in the community is through ritual, as indicated above. Indeed, according to Mbiti, "In African religion there is more *action* for peace and less *talk* about it."[13] He explains that peace is not taken for granted in African religion, for conflict is inevitable between persons, within families, and among communities and peoples. However, religion provides a means of dealing with discord when it does arise, particularly in the profound symbolic significance of ritual.

For example, among the thousands of rituals that are said to take place daily across Africa, Mbiti draws upon one example practised by the Luo and Maasai peoples of Kenya, as recorded by David Shenk. When disputes arose between these peoples, the elders from both sides met to agree on the need and satisfactory terms for peace. Then men, women, and children from both communities convened on the border where the conflict took place. They chopped down trees whose sap is used as poison for arrow tips, and used these trees to erect a fence along the common border. They then placed their weapons of warfare along the fence, which served as a symbol of the war that had divided them. A black dog was laid across the fence and cut into two, so its blood flowed through the fence onto the ground on both sides of the fence. Then the mothers who were nursing would exchange their babies across the fence, so that Maasai mothers nursed Luo babies and vice versa. The respective elders would pray, beseeching God to bless the covenant of peace, and the participants pronounced curses on anyone who crossed the fence to do evil. Hence Shenk concludes,

> The covenant had united the two sides in a bond of peace . ....
> The evil (*enmity*) of the societies, as it were, had been vicariously cleansed through the sacrificial death of the dog. The blood had transformed the war barrier into a sign of peace. The warring parties had become brothers (*and sisters*) by suckling one another's babies.[14]

This example further illustrates the central role of covenants in African societies, as a third means of promoting and sustaining peaceful relations in various human interactions: for instance, marriage, adopting children or other people, borrowing property, arranging employment, or settling disputes. The purpose of such covenants is outlined as follows:

> Covenants serve as preventative measures against the threat to peace and tranquillity. They cement the parties involved into a mystical relationship. They carry obligations of giving and receiving. Their intention is to cultivate peace, good relations, ties, mutuality, friendship, respect and love between people, between people and nature, and between people and spiritual realities (God, divinities and spirits, as the case may be).[15]

Covenants thus carry deep significance in that they establish profound relationships apart from kinship ties, and they are believed to affect the entire community. Moreover, covenants are said to be witnessed and approved by all, including the living-dead and God; to be binding, for breaking a covenant invites a curse upon oneself; and to be everlasting. Thus they are understood to recognize and to recreate one's original ontological unity with God and with humanity. They can only be established where there is openness and transparency, and where they are sought in the case of relational breakdown, restitution is required before establishing the covenant. Finally, covenants require sacrifice, in order to safeguard life through solidifying the

Amani ya Juu ("A Higher Peace")

community, and they are sealed through feasting together as a form of communion and celebration of life in community.[16]

These three means for promoting peace—prayer, rituals, and covenants—are clearly interrelated and certainly intrinsic to African communities. Without a doubt, peace and reconciliation are traditionally understood to originate with God, and to consist in harmony within and among human communities, with the natural realm and with the spiritual realm. The question that necessarily arises is whether these aspects of traditional African thought are relevant to issues of peace and reconciliation in modern Africa. As Aylward Shorter notes, there is a distinct difference in social scale between traditional African contexts, where reconciliation was sought in family feuds, clan disputes, and warring neighbours and communities, and contemporary contexts where it is sought in national, regional, and international conflicts.[17] While one must guard against making facile applications of traditional thought to contemporary situations, it is nonetheless salutary to consider how traditional African concepts and practices of reconciliation may inform peace processes today, particularly at grassroots levels. Before exploring one such community at the grassroots level, it remains to provide a synopsis of reconciliation as interpreted and applied in Christian tradition.

Reconciliation in Christian Thought

In a real sense, peace and reconciliation form fundamental themes running throughout the whole Bible. From the first chapters of Genesis with the account of strife entering the peace-full garden of Eden, to the last chapters of Revelation with the final vision of the new heaven and the new earth, the entire sweep of the biblical narrative concerns reconciliation: between God and humanity, among humans, and with the cosmos. For example, the prophet Isaiah proclaims a vision in which a descendant of David, filled with the Spirit of the Lord, would rule the earth and overcome the strife between all adversaries, human and animal, like the wolf and lamb, leopard and goat, and poisonous snake and child (Isa. 11:1–9). Moreover, Christians interpret Isaiah's vision of the "Prince of Peace" (Isa. 9:6) to be fulfilled in Jesus, who declared among his teachings on the kingdom of God, "Blessed are the peacemakers, for they will be called children of God" (Matt. 5:9).[18] From the angelic annunciation of his birth, saying "Peace on earth," to his final blessing on earth, "Peace I leave with you; my peace I give to you" (John 14:27), Jesus's life proclaimed peace with God, others, and nature.[19] Thus notions of peace and reconciliation are elemental to biblical faith.

Nonetheless, the actual word "to reconcile" (Greek, *katallassein*) is used only thirteen times in the New Testament, and exclusively in the Pauline letters. The Greek term means to make peace after a time of war, yet the concept of reconciliation in Pauline thought evidently functions on three levels: 1) a christological level, with God reconciling the world through Christ (Rom. 5:11); 2) an ecclesiological level, with Christ reconciling Jew and Greek (Eph. 2:12–16); and 3) a cosmic level, with Christ reconciling all of creation unto himself (Col. 1:19–20) and also entrusting this ministry of reconciliation to the church (2 Cor. 5:11–21).[20] Thus the New Testament concept of reconciliation is broad, yet it is summarized well as follows: "Reconciliation is the altering of the state of enmity and conflict against one another, and especially against God, into a relationship of fellowship (*koinonia*) with God and with others, including the environment."[21]

In the long history of theological reflection on reconciliation, there is no single Christian understanding of the concept since it varies somewhat according to context and circumstances.[22] In-depth analysis lies beyond the present scope; therefore, this discussion is primarily informed by Robert Schreiter, a key thinker on the subject of Christian ministries of reconciliation today. Schreiter's main contention is that "*reconciliation is more a spirituality than a strategy.*"[23] He acknowledges that specific tasks and measurable outcomes are necessary in any process of reconciliation, yet he insists that the process cannot be reduced to problem-solving strategies. Instead, he claims,

> What undergirds a successful process of reconciliation is a spirituality, a view of the world that recognizes and responds to God's reconciling action in that world. That is why reconciliation is largely discovered rather than achieved. We experience God's justifying and reconciling activity in our own lives and in our own communities, and it is from that experience that we are able to go forth in a ministry of reconciliation. Thus, reconciliation becomes a way of life, not just a set of discrete tasks to be performed and completed.[24]

In developing this approach, Schreiter calls for two faces of reconciliation: social and spiritual. Social reconciliation involves providing structures and processes for a strife-torn society to be recreated as truthful and just. It requires dealing with the past, punishing wrongdoers, and providing reparation wherever possible to those offended. It also requires creating a secure environment so that an atmosphere of trust, necessary to civil society, can be re-established.

Spiritual reconciliation involves "rebuilding shattered lives so that social reconciliation becomes a reality."[25] While social reconciliation seeks to create conditions for fostering reconciliation, these conditions of themselves cannot effect it. That is to say, the state can establish commissions to investigate wrongdoings, offer amnesty, or punish offenders, yet it cannot legislate healing, forgiveness, and reconciliation. Hence secular organizations often turn to their religious counterparts for assistance with the spiritual dimensions of peace processes. Yet even where indigenous cultures and Christian communities offer means of reconciliation, Schreiter laments that it remains "an elusive spiritual practice."[26]

He therefore advocates an integrated approach to reconciliation in terms of both *spirituality* and *strategies*. Drawing upon biblical analysis, particularly from Paul's teaching on reconciliation, plus theological reflection upon years of ministry experience within conflict-ridden zones, Schreiter offers a framework of five central points on the Christian ministry of reconciliation. His first, most fundamental premise is that "*reconciliation is the work of God, who initiates and completes in us reconciliation through Christ.*"[27] Of course people are involved in the process, yet ultimately reconciliation is not a human achievement but the work of God's grace within us.

Schreiter stresses that God typically initiates this work of reconciliation in the lives of the victims. While one might expect that reconciliation would begin with repentance on the part of the wrongdoers, experience shows that these offenders rarely acknowledge what they have done of their own accord. Instead, Schreiter observes,

> God begins with the victim, restoring to the victim the humanity which the wrongdoer has tried to wrest away or to destroy. This restoration of humanity might be considered the very heart of reconciliation. The experience of reconciliation is the experience of grace—the restoration of one's damaged humanity in a life-giving relationship with God.[28]

The wrongdoer, then, is often called to repentance and forgiveness through the victim's experience of reconciliation. Thus, contrary to some literature on peace and reconciliation, Schreiter maintains that repentance and forgiveness are not preconditions for reconciliation, but rather consequences of it.

The second main point, highlighted above, is that "reconciliation is more a spirituality than a strategy." Schreiter argues that if reconciliation is quintessentially God's work, and we are but "ambassadors for Christ" (2 Cor. 5:20), then reconciliation primarily entails cultivating a relationship with God through which he can effect reconciliation. Schreiter explains,

> That relationship [with God] expresses itself in spiritual practices that create space for truth, for justice, for healing, and for new possibilities. Such practices lead to creating communities of memory, safe places to explore and untangle a painful past, and the cultivation of truth-telling to overcome the lies of injustice and wrongdoing. They lead also to creating communities of hope, where a new future might be imagined and celebrated.[29]

He then notes that reconciled victims often receive a call or vocation to become healers of others, including victims and wrongdoers.

The integration of spirituality and strategies is crucial, for while Schreiter underlines that cultivating and practising such spirituality is essential to reconciliation, he also points out the need for strategies. The first step, in his view, is to create the conditions for fostering reconciliation by establishing communities of memory, of hope, and of safety, where trust can be rediscovered. Among the specific strategies he outlines for promoting reconciliation are "the discernment of similarities and differences between individual and social reconciliation, the promotion of truth-telling and forgiveness, the use of ritual moments, and practices of peace-making."[30] Reconciliation, experienced individually and in small communities, then leads to further action in the realm of social reconciliation such as advocacy for justice in the legal and political structures.

Schreiter's remaining points can only be listed within the present constraints. His third point is that this experience of reconciliation transforms both victim and wrongdoer into a new creation (2 Cor. 5:17). Fourth, the process of reconciliation that creates this new community is grounded in the passion, death, and resurrection of Jesus Christ. Finally, he acknowledges that ultimately the process of reconciliation will only be fulfilled eschatologically, when God reconciles all of the cosmos in Christ.[31] While Schreiter is but one voice in the contemporary field of theological reflection on peace and reconciliation, he provides a clear framework for analyzing ministries of reconciliation in various contexts of the world today.

Reconciliation Lived Out in Nairobi Today: *Amani ya Juu*

Following the brief synopsis of reconciliation in Christian tradition, the question returned to is whether there is any indication of such reconciliation being lived out within East Africa today. If so, is there evidence that traditional African concepts and practices of reconciliation inform such peace processes, particularly at grassroots levels? This section explores these questions through a brief case study of one particular community of refugee women in Nairobi: *Amani ya Juu*. Aside from the limited literature yet available on this particular ministry in print and on its website,[32] qualitative data were collected through participant observation, individual interviews with the two leaders and three refugee women, and one focus group with seven refugee women.[33]

"Sowing peace through the eye of a needle" forms the slogan for *Amani ya Juu* Foundation, a non-profit organization for African women affected by wars and ethnic conflict. Significantly, the founder and director is American missionary Becky Chinchen, who, together with her husband Del and four daughters, became a refugee herself in West Africa. Following many years of ministry in Liberia, the Chinchens finally fled in 1992 when Liberia's civil war encroached upon their community and local Liberians urged that they accompany them in escaping to Ivory Coast. Becky left first with their daughters, and was only reunited with Del a month later. Together they were in and out of Liberia over the following years before the escalation in war prevented their return. In the process they suffered great loss—security, stability, close friends killed in the conflict, their ministry, and almost all their possessions.[34]

After tasting the trauma of countless refugee women across the continent of Africa, Becky arrived in Nairobi deeply burdened for the plight of these women. Hence in 1996, she invited three refugee women to her home and taught them to sew placemats, in hopes of helping them support themselves economically as well as discipling them in their Christian faith. From these humble beginnings, Amani ya Juu has grown to over one hundred women from numerous ethnic groups across eastern, central, and western Africa.[35] While the main centre is located in Nairobi, sister centres have been established in Rwanda, Burundi, Uganda, and Liberia, and sister partnerships with other women's projects have developed across Nairobi (in Eastleigh, Korogocho, and Gituamba), across Kenya (in Kajiado, Wajir, and Kakuma Refugee Camp), and across Africa (Rwanda, Burundi, Uganda, and Liberia).

According to its mission statement, "Amani ya Juu (meaning 'higher peace' in Swahili) is a holistic ministry developing African refugee women in both sewing/ marketing skills as well as in their spiritual growth."[36] With the acquired economic skills, the women are enabled to support their families and eventually to repatriate to their home countries, if possible, to begin their own businesses. With the discipleship programs of daily worship and prayer and weekly Bible studies, these women from many ethnic societies "grow in the Christian characteristics of love, peace and reconciliation."[37] Thus their motto, "sowing peace" or "sowing reconciliation," truly captures the heart of their vision for ministry among refugee women.

As these women together learn and live out reconciliation in Nairobi, are there any indications of their understanding and experience being informed by concepts of reconciliation in African and in Christian tradition, as discussed above? Without a doubt, this dual heritage forms the matrix in which Amani ya Juu has grown and flourished. One illustration alone suffices to demonstrate how African tradition and the Christian faith together enlighten and enliven this ministry of reconciliation.

The central symbol of Amani ya Juu consists of an artistic, colourful quilt displayed in the chapel: the "Unity Quilt." Each panel depicts and celebrates a traditional reconciliation ritual from particular people groups in their representative countries. Yet despite these rich resources from across the continent, the traditional methods of reconciliation have not always been effective, as the refugee women's experience attests. Hence the lower right panel depicts a "broken Africa," illustrating the continent still plagued with conflict, and the resulting question, "Is there a more lasting solution?" As the women explain,

> The dancing woman who is pointing to the cross is celebrating the work of Christ on the cross which has reconciled us to God and given us a higher, more lasting peace (Amani ya Juu) that transcends all tribal and cultural differences. Once we are reconciled to God each of us are able to experience genuine forgiveness and reconciliation with one another. The love of Christ, as displayed through His sacrifice on the cross and experienced in our hearts, is able to bring permanent hope and peace to Africa.[38]

Besides this powerful visual symbol, the qualitative data reveal further evidence of the refugee women's experience of reconciliation being shaped by the dual heritage of African religion and Christian tradition. As in the Unity Quilt itself, however, these two traditions are interwoven so closely in the fabric of community life that it would be a disservice to rend them apart. Hence while Schreiter's theological reflections provide a framework for analysis, both African and Christian traditions are clearly entwined in this particular ministry of reconciliation.

To begin with, Schreiter's call for the two faces of reconciliation, social and spiritual, is certainly borne out by the ministry of *Amani ya Juu*. Definitely the process of establishing peace in this context begins with the spiritual dimension of "rebuilding shattered lives," so that social reconciliation might ensue. Virtually every refugee woman comes to *Amani ya Juu* with her life in shreds from the very circumstances they have faced: civil war, ethnic conflict, exile, poverty, sexual abuse, abandonment, loss, and violence of all kinds. One respondent took hours to narrate her story, scarcely coherent in her attempt to speak the pain of abandonment as a baby, physical and emotional abuse as a fostered child, rape and enforced abortion as a teenager, dire medical conditions as a result, and the emotional, economic, and sexual vulnerability of fleeing the situation alone to become a refugee in a foreign land. Hence she relates her response to a European woman who visited and took her photograph in a refugee camp: "Don't give me money—I want your warm greeting, and tell me that one day I will make it, I will be somebody, a human being."[39]

Surely Schreiter is right in pointing out that the first step towards reconciliation amid such tragic life experiences is to establish communities of safety, where trust can be rediscovered; communities of memory, where the lies imbibed from violators may be overcome with truth, thereby restoring one's human dignity; and communities of hope, where new possibilities can be envisioned. This is certainly the vision and the reality of *Amani ya Juu*, as articulated by the leaders and the refugee women. Becky Chinchen, the

founding director, outlines many challenges that the refugee women face, including the following:

> As refugees you don't know who you can trust—you can no longer trust your neighbour because who you thought was your friend and neighbour turned out to be your enemy. You have to look after your children, to make sure that they get food and security. You have to be strong because there is nobody else. There are probably family members who have been killed and so you've got the emotional pain of the tragedies you've seen and there is no one you've been able to talk to.[40]

Chinchen underlines how difficult it is for the refugee women to feel safe and to heal in such situations. She explains, therefore,

> You need a safe environment where you can come and just be. Sometimes you cannot share right away, that comes after time. You need to be in a place where you know you are going to be accepted no matter who you are, you are going to be loved, you can be a little bit protected where you know your life isn't going to be threatened, and you are going to have the support group to come around you. Even if it's just being with you—sometimes it's not sharing, it's just knowing that your sisters are there and they care about you.[41]

The first step towards reconciliation amid such tragic life experiences is to establish communities of safety, where trust can be rediscovered, and communities of memory, where the lies imbibed from violators may be overcome with truth.

The reality of this safe community of loving acceptance and mutual support is confirmed through participant observation and through the individual and group interviews conducted at *Amani ya Juu*. For example, a Rwandan refugee woman admitted, "Through the problems I went through I felt like God had forgotten me." Therefore, she acknowledged, "It makes it difficult to love your neighbour, you feel like you are incomplete. ... It was difficult for me to embrace somebody." Yet she went on to speak of coming to know God and receiving his love through the community at *Amani ya Juu*:

> Before salvation you cannot have that kind of love like the one we have here at *Amani*; because we know God, we love each other, and it doesn't matter where we have come from, that love comes automatically to our hearts and spills over to our friends. Before I knew God, since I was an orphan without siblings, I felt like God had forgotten me. But when I came to know that God loves me and he has given me sisters like these, I decided to accept Jesus as my personal saviour because he has loved me and given me sisters and others who are like my children. I have love for them, the love that comes from our heavenly Father.[42]

Likewise another refugee explains what she has gained through her experience at *Amani ya Juu*:

> It's not just to get an income but I have seen spiritually the way people love one another, the way they welcome you, and I really felt comforted in my heart. I used to cry always when someone asked me about what I have passed through, but through devotions and Bible study together I become strong. And when I see my sisters

sharing their problems, and I share with them ... I thank God for that.[43]

In addition to establishing safe communities for truth-telling and solidarity, Schreiter calls for particular strategies to promote reconciliation, such as the use of ritual moments and practices of peace-making. One striking example from *Amani ya Juu*, which again fuses African and biblical traditions, is a simple ritual practised daily called "passing the peace." Each morning the women begin their day together with half an hour of worship and prayer. They then "pass the peace" before proceeding to their respective work stations. This ritual consists in elaborate greetings with warm smiles and laughter (and sometimes tears), lengthy handshakes and embraces, plus speaking a word of peace to every other woman present. Not only are such greetings inherent in African cultures, but this particular practice is undoubtedly enriched by Christian tradition, especially in its context following daily worship and prayer.

Reflecting on the practice, one focus-group participant acknowledged, "It's only peace from above which makes us to be united and the prayer of each day which makes us to be strong." She went on to describe the greeting "Peace be with you" as "that kind of message that refreshes. It is like having a cold shower in hot season, it is so refreshing; it makes one strong." She then traced the greeting to Old Testament practice and particularly to "the word of Jesus" both before his death and after his resurrection, as indicated in her conclusion:

> So it's a gift from God . ... For example when Jesus came to the disciples they were heartbroken, though they were praying. But immediately he said, "Peace be with you," and they were awed. It is a strong word, how will I say it? It's like the foundation of our life.

Having explained the significance of the greeting, she then related what the ritual of

CRUX: Fall 2012/Vol. 48, No. 3

"passing the peace" meant to her personally:

> It is out of that love that I want to pass it to another person. Meaning that I do not want to keep it to myself, I want to share it with another person, so that they can benefit from it. It is a free gift from God, and I want to give that gift to another person so that it can be passed on down. Then we can make a difference wherever we are, or wherever we are going. And it's my hope one day maybe the world will be a better place, so that people can say, "Those people have peace, look at they way they are smiling." It is something inside, it's not forced.[44]

This refugee woman's comment leads to the final consideration regarding the ministry of reconciliation at *Amani ya Juu*—namely, social reconciliation. One may not expect that one community of a few dozen poor refugee women in Nairobi would be able to impact social structures to recreate more just and humane societies in East Africa and elsewhere. Yet early indications are that they are indeed having some impact in this regard, both in Nairobi and beyond. A few examples must suffice at present. First, through the success of the ministry among women at *Amani ya Juu*, a new program has been launched called *Amani Watoto* ("Children of Peace"). Since children are the future of Africa, the aim of this program is to work against the ethnic stereotypes and violence in African communities by instilling in children "the values of God's love and acceptance for one another, regardless of race or ethnic group." The program involves day camps for children, as well as taking the message of God's peace into local schools, orphanages, and refugee camps. In sum, the rationale is as follows:

> Children who are exposed to these Kingdom truths early, when values are formed, can become

potential agents of God's peace, reconciliation and transformation in Africa. Employing this proactive strategy for peace can stem tribal conflicts and wars in Africa.[45]

A second tangible indication of *Amani ya Juu* having impact beyond its immediate community stems from the emphasis placed upon giving to others. While refugees typically, and understandably, scrap for resources in order to survive, these refugee women willingly give to others from their profits, however meagre. One poignant example again reflects African tradition: when a woman sets up a new home, a neighbouring woman will often carry coals from her own fire to help the new one begin cooking. In like manner, the women from the original *Amani ya Juu* in Nairobi donated the proceeds from a box of their products to help the women setting up a sister centre in Rwanda. These Rwandan women were so touched by the gesture, that they in turn sent a small delegation to Bujumbura, Burundi, to donate some of their own products to this next fledgling centre. At the grassroots level, then, this message of "a higher peace" has had a ripple effect in the centres and partnerships previously mentioned across Nairobi, Kenya, and Africa.

Finally, the ministry of reconciliation at *Amani ya Juu* has captured the attention of others who are in positions of influence when it comes to transforming political, economic, legal, and other social structures. For example, in 2004, the women were visited by Franklin Graham, the president and CEO of Samaritan's Purse and the Billy Graham Evangelistic Association. Shortly after, they were visited by ten wives of US congressmen, including the wife of the speaker of the house. One of the outcomes of this visit is that *Amani ya Juu* contributed a replica of the Unity Quilt to the former US President and Nobel Peace Prize winner Jimmy Carter. The quilt currently hangs in the Carter Center, where it has the potential to inspire many human rights activists and organizations. Thus in less than a few decades, *Amani ya Juu* has developed a ministry of reconciliation that fosters spiritual and social reconciliation, with tangible outcomes across the continent of Africa and beyond.

Conclusion

In view of the current crisis of refugees in Africa, it is imperative to consider the plight—and the potential—of refugees, particularly refugee women. From the context of Eastern Africa, this article has explored the theme of reconciliation as it is being lived out by the women of *Amani ya Juu* in Nairobi, Kenya. The overriding purpose has not been to critique this ministry of reconciliation, per se; hence within the present constraints, the discussion has not presented the inevitable challenges that arise within this ministry. Rather, the focus has been on exploring ways in which African and Christian traditions are interwoven in the concepts and practices of peace and reconciliation. Clearly, this dual heritage inspires and informs the spirituality of reconciliation these women evidence—that is, how they understand and experience reconciliation, how that reconciliation becomes a key to new possibilities for living, and how these new ways of living are shared with others.

First and foremost, African and biblical traditions converge in the fundamental insight that peace and reconciliation originate with God, and are only possible through God's grace at work in and through the human community. Certainly this foundational theme undergirds the entire ministry of *Amani ya Juu*, as manifested by the leaders, the literature, and the ladies themselves. Second, both religious traditions highlight the need for the internal and external, or the individual and social dimensions of peace and reconciliation. The *Amani ya Juu* women manifest these dimensions to varying degrees, from the personal care given to incoming refugees traumatized by their experience of suffering injustice, to their communal efforts to

proclaim "peace from above" across Nairobi, Kenya, Africa, and beyond. Third, the dual heritage reveals the crucial importance of prayer, ritual, and covenant in relation to fostering peace and reconciliation. Once again, all these aspects have been manifested in the ministry of reconciliation among these refugee women. While they do not overtly use the term "covenant," the core commitment to Christ underlying the ministry, plus the common identity and mutual commitment demonstrated by the women, justify the term "covenant community" in relation to *Amani ya Juu*. Finally, and most significantly, African and Christian traditions are interwoven in the very fabric of their community life, from the symbolic Unity Quilt that displays their vision, to the spirituality and strategies that demonstrate their ministry of reconciliation.

The *Amani ya Juu* women definitely exemplify Jesus's affirmation, "Blessed are the peacemakers, for they will be called children of God." As these women symbolically share their "coals," they not only establish new centres of peace across the conflict-ridden continent of Africa, they also offer genuine insights into living out reconciliation for all those committed to seeking "peace from above." In so doing, they embody this vital theme of reconciliation in Christ so central to the spiritual theology of James Houston. ✗

Notes

1. This is the most common rendition heard orally. One African proverbs website (http://www.afriprov.org/index.php/african-proverbs-calendar/48-2011cal/560-feb2011.html) has it thus: "When elephants fight the grass (reeds) gets hurt."
2. Robert J. Schreiter, *The Ministry of Reconciliation: Spirituality and Strategies* (Maryknoll, NY: Orbis Books, 1998), 25–26.
3. Ibid., 29.
4. John Mbiti, "Peace and Reconciliation in African Religion and Christianity," *Dialogue & Alliance* 7, no. 1 (Spring/Summer 1993): 17.
5. Schreiter, *Ministry of Reconciliation*, 5.
6. Laurenti Magesa, *African Religion: The Moral Traditions of Abundant Life* (Maryknoll, NY: Orbis Books, 1997), 234.
7. G.C. Harris, *Casting Out Anger: Religion Among the Taita of Kenya* (Cambridge: Cambridge University

Press, 1978), 28; quoted in Magesa, *African Religion*, 235.

8. Harris, *Casting Out Anger*, 46; quoted in Magesa, *African Religion*, 235.

9. See also Aylward Shorter, "Reconciliation in African Traditional Spirituality," in *Spirituality and Reconciliation*, Tangaza Occasional Papers, no. 4 (Nairobi: Paulines Publications Africa, 1997), 7–8.

10. Mbiti, "Peace and Reconciliation," 18.

11. Ibid., 19.

12. Ibid.

13. Ibid., 22; emphasis original.

14. David W. Shenk, *Peace and Reconciliation in Africa* (Nairobi: Uzima Press, 1983), 68–69; quoted in Mbiti, "Peace and Reconciliation," 22–23, with Mbiti's parenthetical notes.

15. Mbiti, "Peace and Reconciliation," 25.

16. Shenk, *Peace and Reconciliation*, 72–74, in Mbiti, "Peace and Reconciliation," 26. See also E. Bolaji Idowu, *Oledumare: God in Yoruba Belief* (London: Longmans, 1962), 149–50.

17. Shorter, "Reconciliation," 13–14.

18. All Scripture quotations are taken from the NRSV.

19. Mbiti, "Peace and Reconciliation," 28.

20. Robert J. Schreiter, "Reconciliation," in *Dictionary of Mission: Theology, History, Perspectives* (Maryknoll, NY: Orbis Books, 1997), 379–80.

21. Philip Potter, "Mission as Reconciliation in the Power of the Spirit: Impulses from Canberra," *International Review of Mission* 80, nos. 319–320 (1991): 309.

22. For example, see the various perspectives reflected in Gregory Baum and Harold Wells, eds., *The Reconciliation of Peoples: Challenge to the Churches* (Maryknoll, NY: Orbis Books, 1997).

23. Robert J. Schreiter, *Reconciliation: Mission and Ministry in a Changing Social Order* (Maryknoll, NY: Orbis Books, 1992), 60; emphasis original.

24. Ibid.

25. Schreiter, *Ministry of Reconciliation*, 4.

26. Ibid.

27. Ibid., 14; emphasis original.

28. Ibid., 15.

29. Ibid., 16.

30. Ibid.

31. Ibid., 17–19.

32. See http://www.amaniafrica.org.

33. All interviews were tape recorded, transcribed, and analyzed using the computer software NVivo 6. While permission was obtained to quote by name the founder and director, Becky Chinchen, and the ministry coordinator, Margie Koech, data presented from the refugee women remain anonymous.

34. Becky Chinchen, interview by author (Nairobi: March 15, 2004).

35. Personal communication with Cathie Burke, *Amani ya Juu* staff, October 26, 2012.

36. *Amani ya Juu* Mission Statement, made available to the author by Becky Chinchen.

37. Ibid.

38. *Amani ya Juu* website, http://www.amaniafrica.org/about.php. See "Our Unity Quilt" and "Dancing African Women."

39. Interview by author (Nairobi: March 18, 2004).

40. Becky Chinchen, interview by author (Nairobi: March 15, 2004).

41. Ibid.

42. Interview by author (Nairobi: March 16, 2004).

43. Ibid.

44. Focus Group by author (Nairobi: March 18, 2004).

45. *Amani Watoto* brochure. See also http://www.amaniafrica.org/peace.php, "Amani ya Watoto.